Getting Ready *for* Baby

Getting Ready *for* Baby

50 Fast and Easy Sewing Projects for
Grandmothers, Aunts, and Mothers-to-Be

···

ANN POE *and* KANDY SCHNEIDER

CB

CONTEMPORARY BOOKS

Library of Congress Cataloging-in-Publication Data

Poe, Ann.
    Getting ready for baby : sewing, quilting, and applique projects /
Ann Poe, Kandy Schneider.
       p.   cm.
    ISBN 0-8092-2904-8
    1. Textile Crafts.   2. Needlework—Patterns.   3. Infants'
clothing.   4. Infants' supplies.   I. Schneider, Kandy   II. Title.
TT699.P64   1997
746—dc21   97-51234
                                       CIP

Cover design by Kim Bartko
Cover photograph by Sharon Hoogstraten
Interior design by Mary Lockwood
Interior illustrations by Shauna Mooney Kawasaki, with digital color enhancement
by Amy Yu Ng
Interior photography by Sharon Hoogstraten

Published by Contemporary Books
A division of NTC/Contemporary Publishing Group, Inc.
4255 West Touhy Avenue, Lincolnwood (Chicago), Illinois 60646-1975 U.S.A.
Printed in the United States of America
International Standard Book Number: 0-8092-2904-8
99 00 01 02 03 04 QB 19 18 17 16 15 14 13 12 11 10 9 8 7 6 5 4 3 2 1

to David, Christopher, and Elizabeth Poe
to Stephen, Jason, Christopher, and Stephanie Schneider

A Child of Happiness always seems like an old soul living in a new body, and her face is very serious until she smiles, and then the sun lights up the world. . . . Children of Happiness always look not quite the same as other children. They have strong, straight legs and walk with purpose. They laugh as do all children, and they play as do all children, they talk child talk as do all children, but they are different, they are blessed, they are special, they are sacred.

Anne Cameron

Contents

Introduction

This book is for grandmothers, aunts, mothers-to-be, and anyone else who wants to make something special for a new baby. It will help if you know a little bit about sewing, but you needn't be an expert. If you can set up your sewing machine and sew a straight seam, you'll do fine.

The quilts and projects are designed to be easy and fun to do. The techniques are basic, and the instructions are written with beginners in mind. These projects are forgiving, so don't worry if your sewing skills are rusty. The finished item will still look good, and besides, Mother and Baby will be too busy cooing at one another to notice any imperfections.

These projects can be made quickly, too. If you have all your fabric and supplies on hand, most items can be finished in a weekend, even the quilts. If you want super-quick results, try the bath set (page 47) or sacque set (page 23) first.

Throughout the book, there are helpful tips and options for easy variations—even experienced seamstresses are likely to pick up some new shortcuts and ideas. Freedom of choice is encouraged—do as much hand quilting as you like, or embellish and trim Baby's outfit to match one of Mother's. Just remember that babies like to pull off buttons and swallow them, so be wary of trims that Baby's fingers can grab.

The sections on Getting Ready to Sew (page xi) and Sewing and Quilting Basics (pages 101 and 107) are a handy reference for the techniques you'll use in making the projects in this book. Take time to read them, or at least be aware of what is included. When several coordinating fabrics are used in a project, fabrics are labeled A, B, C, etc., so that you can duplicate the item in the photo more easily. Additional fabric suggestions are included in each chapter.

We hope you enjoy making these projects as much as we did. May your babies be healthy, joyful, and abundantly blessed.

Ann Poe
Kandy Schneider

Before You Begin

The items in this book are easy-to-sew projects. It will help if you can sew a little, but you don't need a lot of experience. If you can turn on your sewing machine and sew a straight line, this book is for you. Most beginners can make any of these projects in a weekend.

Getting Ready to Sew

Before you begin, organize your supplies. The directions assume that you have the following tools and materials on hand.

Sewing machine—A basic zigzag machine in good working order is fine. Make sure the machine has been recently oiled, the bobbin case is lint free, and the needle is brand-new. Along with a regular *zigzag foot*, which has an opening to allow for the zigzag motion of the needle, you will want to have these feet on hand:

> *zipper foot*—used to sew bias strips around cording or piping

> *rolled-edge hem foot*—folds under the raw edge and stitches it in place in one step

> *overcast foot*—used with the overcast stitch to cover a raw edge. If your machine doesn't have this foot, zigzag over the raw edge.

Rotary cutter—Used with a ruler and cutting mat, this is a useful tool for trimming edges and for slicing through several layers of fabric at once. The cutter blade is round and very sharp, so keep the blade in the "closed" position when not in use.

Cutting mat—The mat goes under the fabric and protects the surface underneath. Mats come in many sizes and are made from special materials that can stand repeated cutting without damaging the cutter blade.

Scissors—Use good-quality dressmaker shears for cutting fabric. Keep a second, inexpensive pair on hand for cutting paper. Small embroidery scissors are convenient for clipping threads at the sewing machine.

Ruler—Use a ruler specially made for use with a rotary cutter. Some rulers have a lip on one end; the lip catches the edge of the cutting mat and steadies the ruler.

Thread—Top-quality threads are not prone to breaking; they pass through the sewing machine needle easily and smoothly. Inexpensive threads tend to get fuzzy and knot easily. Choose colors that match or appear neutral against the fabrics you are using.

Needles—Use a size appropriate for the fabric. For sewing 100 percent cotton, for example, size 80/12 universal needle should work. Fine fabrics, such as batiste, require size 70/10; heavier fabrics may require size 90/14. For quilting through several layers, use a needle specifically designed for machine quilting. You should also have an assortment of hand-sewing needles on hand.

Pins—Long straight pins with a large head are easy to see; use them for quilting and working with cotton or heavier fabrics. Brass safety pins are useful for pin-basting quilts; these can be found in most quilting shops. Fine glass-head pins work well on lightweight fabrics.

Choosing Fabric

Sewing is easier with high-quality fabric. The quilting projects in this book are made with 100 percent cotton. Decorator cottons can be harder to work with, as they are more tightly woven and have less ease. They are sometimes too heavy for baby quilts. If you are using a fabric with a one-way design or nap, remember to buy extra.

Choose small prints and pastels or primary colors for baby items. When you need a solid color, choose a mottled color or one that is overprinted with a small design. The overall effect will "read" solid, but the dappled color or subtle design adds extra life and character to the finished project.

Preparing Fabric

Be sure to wash your fabric in soap and hot water before cutting. It's important to wash away any sizing that might irritate Baby's delicate skin. Some soaps will also soften the fabric. Dry the fabric following manufacturer's directions. If you preshrink the fabric, the finished quilt or clothing won't change shape or size when laundered later.

Cutting Fabric

Measuring and cutting fabric strips for quilts is quick and easy when you use a rotary cutter. Fold the fabric (you can fold it twice if needed), keeping selvages together. Square off the end, then cut off strips to the required width.

Trim selvages before cutting out patterns or sewing. Selvages should never be part of a seam allowance.

Note that measurements often are based on fabric width. Feel free to adjust measurements to suit your fabric. In other words, if your fabric is a little narrower or wider than the directions, use the width as is. If the finished project has a lot of fullness, such as a window valance, hamper skirt, or ruffle, a little more or less is unlikely to affect the final appearance.

•shopping tip•

Look for coordinating fabrics. You'll probably want five to seven different fabrics if you're planning to decorate a room. Once you've found what you like, make a list of which fabrics will be used with each project. Now you're ready to add up fabric requirements and go shopping.

Sunshine Accessories
Preparing the Nursery

Add sunshine to Baby's bedroom with a crib quilt and room accessories in lovely pastel colors. The rail fence design is a good pattern for quick strip-piecing. A coordinating dust ruffle and reversible bumper pads complete the crib ensemble. Decorate the rest of the room with matching window valance, lampshade skirt, quick-and-easy covers for tissue box, wastebasket, and clothes hamper.

fabric suggestions

These projects work up well in broadcloth, cotton, calico, gingham, or decorator fabrics. The projects shown use seven coordinating fabrics.

rail fence crib quilt

• •

Finished size is 54" × 44" (135 cm × 110 cm).

Strip-piece the quilt top into three sections, then use flip-and-sew technique to assemble the layers and quilt in one easy step.

•tips•

Cut strips of fabric using a rotary cutter. Cut several at once by layering fabrics carefully, one on top of another.

   Use self-adhesive labels to identify each cut piece on the wrong side. Remove the label just before sewing.

Supplies

Fabric	Piece	Amount
A	top	½ yard (0.5 meter)
B	top	½ yard (0.5 meter)
C	top, binding, center back	2½ yards (2.3 meters)
D	top, border, outside back	2¼ yards (2.1 meters)
¼" (0.75 cm) wide double-faced satin ribbon		4 yards (3.7 meters)
Low-loft polyester batting		45" × 60" (112.5 cm × 150 cm)

Cutting

Fabric	Piece	Cut	Size
A, B, C, D	top	8 strips each	2" × fabric width* (5 cm × fabric width)

Cut the following pieces from the remaining fabric length:

Fabric	Piece	Cut	Size
C	center back	1	25" × 63" (62.5 cm × 157.5 cm)
	binding	2	2" × 58" (5 cm × 145 cm)
		2	2" × 46" (5 cm × 115 cm)
D	outside back	2	11" × 63" (27.5 cm × 157.5 cm)
	border	2	4½" × 46" (11.25 cm × 115 cm)
		2	4½" × 50" (11.25 cm × 125 cm)

*Standard fabric width is 44"–45" (110–112.5 cm).

instructions

1. With right sides together and using a ¼" (0.75 cm) seam allowance, sew strips A, B, C, D together lengthwise in order shown. Press seams toward one edge (fig. 1-1). The strip set is now 6½" (16.25 cm) wide. Repeat to make eight strip sets.

2. Trim selvages. Cut strip sets crosswise to make 6½" (16.25 cm) squares (fig. 1-2). Cut 48 squares.

3. Arrange squares, alternating directions as shown. Sew together four squares to make one four-patch block (fig. 1-3). Repeat to make 12 blocks. To make double crosses as shown in the photo, the two most dominant colors should be on outside strips—positions A and D.

4. If pressed correctly, cross seams will nest easily. Pin carefully at seam for a perfect match. These four-patch blocks should be the same size, so remeasure and trim as needed to make each one uniform. The uniformity is more important than the measurement per se. In other words, if your squares turn out to be 12¼" (30.75 cm) instead of 12½" (31.25 cm), that's OK.

5. Sew blocks together to make three strips of four four-patch blocks (fig. 1-4). Where four-patch blocks are joined, press seams in same direction.

6. Sew outside backs to both sides of center back (fig. 1-5). Press seams toward darker fabric.

•tips•

Make extra squares now (Steps 1 and 2). (One strip will make six squares.) You will need the extra squares later when making the coordinating room accessories (four for the tissue box, fifteen for the valance, four for the headboard).

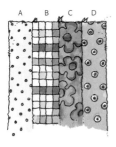

fig. 1-1

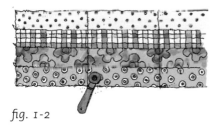

fig. 1-2

fig. 1-3

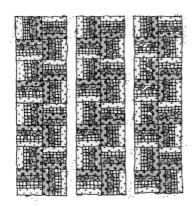

fig. 1-4

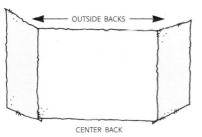

fig. 1-5

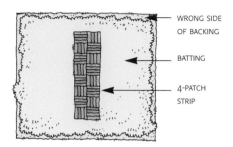

WRONG SIDE
OF BACKING

BATTING

4-PATCH
STRIP

fig. 1-6

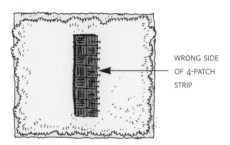

WRONG SIDE
OF 4-PATCH
STRIP

fig. 1-7

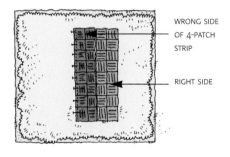

WRONG SIDE
OF 4-PATCH
STRIP

RIGHT SIDE

fig. 1-8

7. Place backing right side down. Center quilt batting on top of backing. Center a four-patch strip, right side up, on top of batting. Measure carefully to make sure it is equidistant from all four edges (fig. 1-6).

8. Place second four-patch strip on top of first, right sides together. Pin all layers together along right hand edge of blocks. Match seams carefully, easing as necessary. Sew through all layers (fig. 1-7). Remove pins, flip open, and press.

9. Place remaining four-patch strip on top of center strip, right sides together. Pin all layers together carefully along left hand edge of center strip, matching block seams, easing as necessary (fig. 1-8). Sew, flip open, and press.

10. Pin 50″ (125 cm) border strips to each side of quilt, right sides together, then sew through all layers. Trim away excess, flip open, and press (fig. 1-9). Add 46″ (115 cm) borders to top and bottom in the same way.

11. Machine quilt through all layers by stitching "in-the-ditch" (see Quilting Basics, page 107). Start in the middle and work toward outside edges, skipping over the seams that have already been stitched. Change direction as you quilt back and forth and up and down. Continue until you have quilted around individual blocks (fig. 1-10).

12. Pin-baste border securely. Quilt in border 1½″ (3.75 cm) away from outer edge of blocks (fig. 1-11).

13. Square up quilt, trimming away excess fabric and batting (fig. 1-12).

14. Fold under ¼″ (0.75 cm) along each long edge of the binding strip; fold in half lengthwise. Press (fig. 1-13).

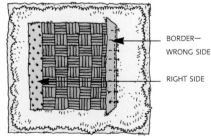

BORDER—
WRONG SIDE

RIGHT SIDE

fig. 1-9

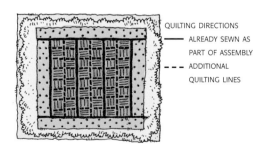

QUILTING DIRECTIONS
——— ALREADY SEWN AS
PART OF ASSEMBLY
- - - ADDITIONAL
QUILTING LINES

fig. 1-10

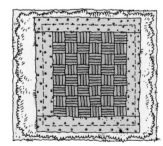

fig. 1-11

15. Pin binding to back of quilt along one side, matching edges. Sew using ¼″ (0.75 cm) seam allowance (fig. 1-14).

16. Fold binding to front, covering raw edge. Pin, then topstitch through all layers. Trim binding even with quilt edges (fig. 1-15). Repeat for other side.

17. Attach binding to back of quilt along top edge as in Step 14, leaving 1″ (2.5 cm) tail at both ends. Fold tails to inside (fig. 1-16), then fold binding over raw edge as in Step 15. Pin to hold, and topstitch through all layers (fig. 1-17). Repeat for bottom edge.

18. Make 18 ribbon bows, each from 6″ (15 cm) length of ribbon. Sew onto quilt by machine, using zigzag stitch and 0 stitch length. Stitch through bow knot and all quilt layers. Stitching will prevent bows from coming untied.

•tip•

Be sure to trim the ribbon ends at an angle to prevent fraying.

fig. 1-12

fig. 1-13

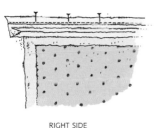

RIGHT SIDE

fig. 1-14

QUILT FRONT—
RIGHT SIDE

fig. 1-15

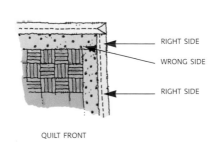

RIGHT SIDE

WRONG SIDE

RIGHT SIDE

QUILT FRONT

fig. 1-16

QUILT FRONT—
RIGHT SIDE

fig. 1-17

bumper pads and headboard pad

Bumper pads are designed to fit three sides of a crib. Complete this set with a headboard pad from page 9.

bumper pads

•option•

Rather than make a separate headboard, cut an additional bumper pad end piece, then proceed as in Steps 1–7.

Supplies

Fabric	Piece	Amount
A	front	1½ yards (1.4 meters)
B	back	1½ yards (1.4 meters)
⅜″ (1 cm) wide grosgrain ribbon		5⅓ yards (5 meters)
High-loft polyester batting*		81″ × 96″ (202.5 cm × 240 cm)

*Includes batting for headboard pad.

Cutting

Fabric	Piece	Cut	Size
A	front	1	11″ × 30″ (27.5 cm × 75 cm)
		2	11″ × 53″ (27.5 cm × 132.5 cm)
B	back	1	11″ × 30″ (27.5 cm × 75 cm)
		2	11″ × 53″ (27.5 cm × 132.5 cm)
Batting		2	11″ × 30″ (27.5 cm × 75 cm)
		4	11″ × 53″ (27.5 cm × 132.5 cm)

instructions

1. Pin batting to wrong side of each bumper front piece. Baste by machine with a long straight stitch, ⅜″ (1 cm) from edge, along all sides. Batting will tend to stretch, so trim as needed after stitching. Repeat for bumper back pieces (fig. 1-18).

2. Trim batting close to seam lines. Pin front side piece to each end of front end piece, right sides together, then sew using ½″ (1.25 cm) seam allowance. Press seams open. Press lightly so as not to flatten batting. Repeat for bumper back (fig. 1-19).

3. Cut 12 ribbon ties, each 16″ (40 cm) long. Fold each ribbon in half, and pin in position along edges of bumper front on right side. Ties will be at top and bottom of each corner, at each seam, and at center of long sides. Pin the ties with the ends pointed toward middle of bumper pad (fig. 1-20).

4. Pin bumper back to bumper front, right sides together, leaving one end open. Sew using a ½" (1.25 cm) seam allowance. Backstitch across ties for reinforcement (fig. 1-21).

5. Turn right side out, being careful not to pull apart batting. Starting at open end, pull through a little bit (about one arm's length) at a time, taking care to grasp both fabric and batting.

6. Close end with ladder stitch (See Sewing Basics, page 101).

7. Machine quilt from top edge to bottom edge as shown. You will need to use a large needle (size 16/100) and a longer stitch length (fig. 1-22).

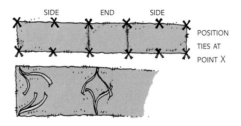

RIGHT SIDE OF FABRIC
STITCHLINE
BATTING
FRONT   BACK

fig. 1-18

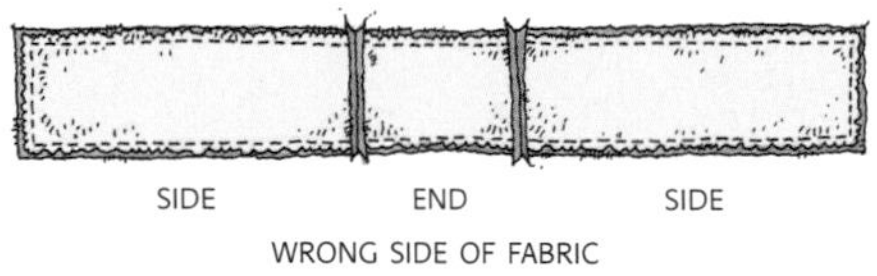

SIDE   END   SIDE
WRONG SIDE OF FABRIC

fig. 1-19

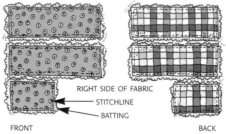

SIDE   END   SIDE

POSITION TIES AT POINT X

fig. 1-20

SEAMLINE

fig. 1-21

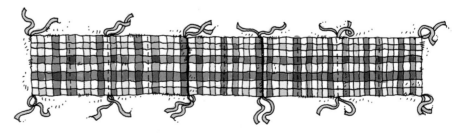

fig. 1-22

headboard pad

Supplies

Fabric	Piece	Amount
D	front	¾ yard (0.75 meter)
B	center back	¾ yard (0.75 meter)
A	outside back	¾ yard (0.75 meter)
1½" (3.75 cm) wide ruffled white eyelet		1½ yards (1.4 meters)
¼" (0.75 cm) wide double-faced satin ribbon		1 yard (1 meter)
⅜" (1 cm) wide grosgrain ribbon		2 yards (1.9 meters)
High-loft polyester batting*		
4 rail fence squares†		

*See Bumper Pads, page 7.   †See Rail Fence Crib Quilt, Steps 1 and 2, page 3.

Cutting

Patterns are provided, beginning on page 115. Using a photocopier, enlarge as directed. Cutting instructions appear on the pattern.

Fabric	Piece	Cut	Size
D	front	1	21" × 31" (52.5 cm × 77.5 cm)
B	center back	1	16" × 21" (40 cm × 52.5 cm)
A	outside back	2	8" × 21" (20 cm × 52.5 cm)
Batting		2	21" × 31" (52.5 cm × 77.5 cm)

instructions

1. Using pattern, cut fabric as directed.

2. With right sides together and using a ¼" (0.75 cm) seam allowance, sew outside backs to each side of center back (fig. 1-23).

3. Use pattern to cut out headboard back and front (fig. 1-24).

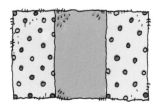

fig. 1-23

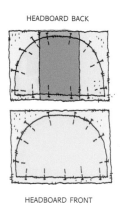

HEADBOARD BACK

HEADBOARD FRONT

fig. 1-24

fig. 1-25

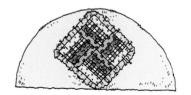

fig. 1-26

4. Make four squares, each 6½″ (16.25 cm) square (see Rail Fence Crib Quilt, Steps 1 and 2, page 3). Then sew squares together to make one four-patch block. Press.

5. With right sides together, pin eyelet around edge of block, beginning at center of one side. Stitch in place (fig. 1-25).

6. Press eyelet away from block; seam will fold under and be pressed toward block. Pin trimmed block onto headboard front, centered and on diagonal as shown. Topstitch in place (fig. 1-26).

7. Pin batting to wrong side of headboard front. Stitch around all sides, ⅜″ (1 cm) from edge. Repeat for headboard back (fig. 1-27).

8. Cut four ties, each 16″ (40 cm) long. Pin two ties to each side of headboard front. Then with right sides together, pin headboard front to headboard back. Sew around edges, keeping ties to inside and leaving an opening on bottom edge for turning. Backstitch over ties to reinforce (fig. 1-28).

9. Turn right side out. Use slipstitch to close opening.

10. Quilt along outside edge of four-patch seam under eyelet (this quilting line will be hidden from view). Then quilt along sides and curved edge of headboard, 1½″ (3.75 cm) from edge.

11. Make five ribbon bows, each from 6″ (15 cm) length of satin ribbon. Sew bows onto four-patch block by machine, using zigzag stitch and 0 stitch length. Stitch through bow knot and all layers (fig. 1-29).

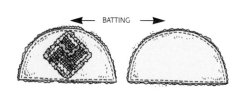

BATTING

fig. 1-27

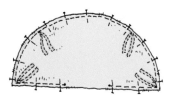

fig. 1-28

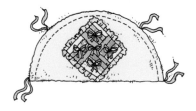

fig. 1-29

dust ruffle

This coordinating dust ruffle is made to fit around the corner posts of the crib.

Supplies

Fabric	Piece	Amount
C	crib ruffle	2¾ yards (2.6 meters)
Muslin	crib deck	1½ yards (1.4 meters)

Cutting

Fabric	Piece	Cut	Size
C	ruffles	6	12″ × 44″ (30 cm × 110 cm)
		4	12″ × 22″ (30 cm × 55 cm)
Muslin	deck	1	29″ × 53″ (72.5 cm × 132.5 cm)

instructions

1. Hem each corner of crib deck on diagonal by turning up ¼″ (0.75 cm), then another ¼″ (0.75 cm), forming a double-fold hem. Press and stitch in place (fig. 1-30).

2. Trim selvages from ruffle ends. For each side section, sew two long pieces and one short piece end to end. For each end section, sew one long piece and one short piece end to end. Press seams open (fig. 1-31).

3. Hem sides of each section by turning up ¼″ (0.75 cm), then ½″ (1.25 cm). Press and stitch in place. Hem bottom edge of each section by turning up ¼″ (0.75 cm), then ¾″ (2 cm). Press and stitch in place. Fold corners at 45° angle to miter (fig. 1-32).

4. Using a long machine basting stitch, sew two lines of stitching along raw edge. Lines should be ⅜″ (1 cm) apart and within seam allowance. Mark center and quarter points, then pull threads to gather fabric (fig. 1-33).

5. With right sides together and raw edges matching, place ruffle sections on top of quilt deck. Distribute fullness evenly and pin carefully to hold gathers in position. Each ruffle section ends at a corner hem. The open corner space permits the completed dust ruffle to fit around the corner posts of the crib (fig. 1-34).

6. Press ruffle so that seam allowances are toward crib deck. Topstitch over seam allowances to strengthen seams (fig. 1-35).

fig. 1-30

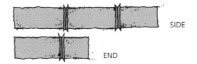

SIDE

END

fig. 1-31

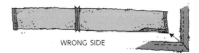

WRONG SIDE

fig. 1-32

fig. 1-33

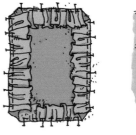

fig. 1-34   *fig. 1-35*

window valance

· ·

This valance is for a 36″ (90 cm) wide window but can easily be altered to fit any window.

Supplies

Fabric	Piece	Amount
E	top and bottom bands	1 yard (1 meter)

15 rail fence squares*

Curtain rod to fit window

*See Rail Fence Crib Quilt, Steps 1 and 2, page 3.

Cutting

Fabric	Piece	Cut	Size
E	top band	1	12″ × 45″ (30 cm × 112.5 cm)
		2	12″ × 23½″ (30 cm × 58.75 cm)
	bottom band	1	5″ × 45″ (12.5 cm × 112.5 cm)
		2	5″ × 23½″ (12.5 cm × 58.75 cm)

instructions

1. Sew rail fence squares end to end, alternating direction of strips in each square (fig. 1-36).

2. Assemble top and bottom bands by sewing a short strip to each end of long strip. Press seams open. Sew bands lengthwise to quilt squares (fig. 1-37).

3. Make double-fold hem on side edges by turning up ¼″ (0.75 cm), then ½″ (1.25 cm). Press and stitch in place (fig. 1-38).

4. Hem bottom edge by turning up ½″ (1.25 cm), then 1″ (2.5 cm). Fold under corners at 45° angle to miter. Press and stitch in place. Hem top edge by turning up ½″ (1.25 cm), then 4″ (10 cm); fold under corners to miter. Press and machine stitch (fig. 1-39).

5. Sew stitching line 2″ (5 cm) from top edge. Insert curtain rod through pocket (fig. 1-40).

fig. 1-36

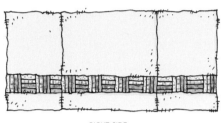
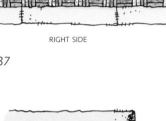

RIGHT SIDE

fig. 1-37

WRONG SIDE

fig. 1-38

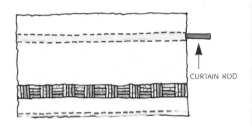

CORNER VIEW

fig. 1-39

CURTAIN ROD

fig. 1-40

•measuring for a window valance•

Measure the window, including the window frame. A ruffled curtain or valance will look best if it is two to three times wider than the window.

Decide on finished top-to-bottom length. Allow 4"–6" (10–15 cm) for top casing and rod pocket and 1½"–3" (3.75–7.5 cm) for bottom hem. The rod pocket should be about an inch wider than the curtain rod to allow room for gathering. A 2" (5 cm) wide pocket will nicely accommodate a standard-size curtain rod.

lampshade skirt

•••

This easy-to-make gathered skirt sits on top of a bedroom lampshade.

Supplies

Fabric	Piece	Amount
D	skirt	¾ yard (0.75 meter)
1½″ (3.75 cm) wide wired-edge ribbon		1½ yards (1.4 meters)
⅛″ (0.5 cm) wide elastic		½ yard (0.5 meter)
Purchased flared lampshade*		

*The lampshade shown is 7″ (17.5 cm) high with a bottom circumference of 35″ (87.5 cm).

Cutting

Fabric	Piece	Cut	Size
D	skirt	2	11″ × 36″ (27.5 cm × 90 cm)

instructions

1. Place skirt pieces right sides together, matching raw edges. Using ¼″ (0.75 cm) seam allowance, stitch together each 11″ (27.5 cm) end. Press seams open (fig. 1-41).

2. Make double-fold hem on top and bottom edges by turning up edges ¼″ (0.75 cm), then ½″ (1.25 cm). Press and stitch in place (fig. 1-42).

3. Mark a line 2″ (5 cm) from top edge on wrong side of fabric. Place elastic along this line, holding it in place with machine zigzag stitch. The stitch acts as a casing for elastic, crossing from edge to edge, but not through it (fig. 1-43).

4. Pull elastic and gather fabric so skirt sits nicely on top of lampshade (fig. 1-44). Overlap ends of elastic and stitch together.

5. Make bow with wired-edge ribbon. Pin in place with brass safety pin.

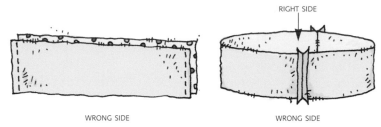

RIGHT SIDE

WRONG SIDE   WRONG SIDE

fig. 1-41

fig. 1-42

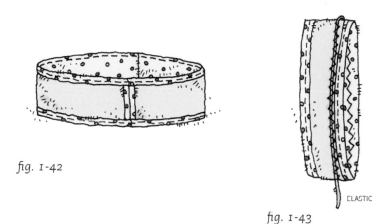

ELASTIC

fig. 1-43

fig. 1-44

•measuring for a flared lampshade cover•

Measure the lampshade from top to bottom edge. Measure around the bottom edge. Prepare a strip of fabric with a length equal to twice the bottom circumference and a width equal to the lampshade height plus 4″ (10 cm). Follow the project instructions on page 14 to finish.

tissue box cover

· ·

This cover will fit a cube-shaped tissue box.

Supplies

Fabric	Piece	Amount
A, D	top	one 6½" square each (one 16.25 cm square each)

Four rail fence squares*

1" (2.5 cm) wide ruffled eyelet	¾ yard (0.75 meter)

*See Rail Fence Crib Quilt, Steps 1 and 2, page 3.

instructions

1. Trace tissue box opening onto wrong side of fabric D (fig. 1-45).

2. Place squares (A, D) right sides together, with traced opening on top. Sew together along drawn line. Cut out opening, leaving ¼" (0.75 cm) seam allowance. Clip seam allowance carefully (fig. 1-46).

3. Pull one square through opening so that it becomes a facing for the other. Press carefully. Round off corners slightly (fig. 1-47).

4. Sew four rail fence squares end to end, alternating direction of strips (fig. 1-48). Join ends to form four sides of box cover (fig. 1-49).

5. With right sides together, pin top to sides, matching corners and centers. Sew around four top edges (fig. 1-50). (Stitch with sides on top and top underneath.)

6. Turn right side out, clipping corners as needed. Sew eyelet to bottom edge, right sides together, raw edges matching (fig. 1-51).

7. Open out eyelet and press toward bottom edge. Topstitch on eyelet as shown (fig. 1-52).

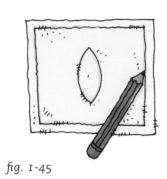

fig. 1-45

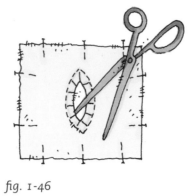

fig. 1-46

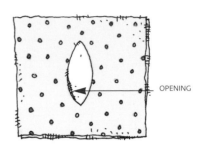

OPENING

fig. 1-47

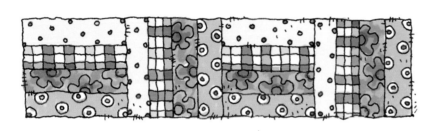

fig. 1-48

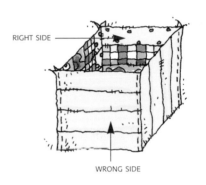

RIGHT SIDE

WRONG SIDE

fig. 1-49

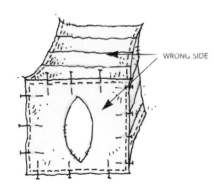

WRONG SIDE

fig. 1-50

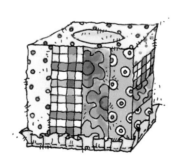

fig. 1-51

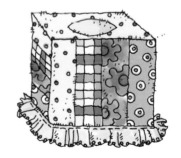

fig. 1-52

•tip•

If the fabric cover is too heavy, use Velcro strips to help support the fabric weight. Stitch Velcro loop strips onto the gathered edge of front and back. Glue Velcro hook strips in position on the hamper or wastebasket.

wastebasket cover

Follow the measuring instructions below to cover any size wastebasket.

Supplies

Fabric	Piece	Amount
F	cover	1 yard (1 meter)
½" (1.25 cm) wide elastic		½ yard (0.5 meter)
1½" (3.75 cm) wide wired-edge ribbon		1½ yards (1.4 meters)
Purchased plastic wastebasket*		

*The wastebasket shown is rectangular-shaped, 13½" (33.75 cm) tall, with a top circumference of 38" (95 cm) and a bottom circumference of 34½" (86.25 cm).

Cutting

Fabric	Piece	Cut	Size
F	cover	2	17" × 40" (42.5 cm × 100 cm)
Elastic	top elastic	1	26" (65 cm)
	bottom elastic	1	28" (70 cm)

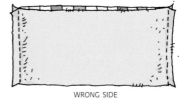

WRONG SIDE

fig. 1-53

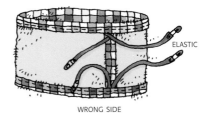

ELASTIC

WRONG SIDE

fig. 1-54

instructions

1. Place cover pieces right sides together, with raw edges matching. Using ½" (1.25 cm) seam allowance, stitch together each 17" (42.5 cm) end. Press seams open (fig. 1-53).

2. Turn under top edge ½" (1.25 cm), then 1" (2.5 cm), to form a casing for elastic. Press and sew, leaving a 2" (5 cm) opening to insert elastic. Repeat for bottom edge (fig. 1-54).

3. Insert elastic in top and bottom casings. Secure ends and close openings with slipstitches. Turn right side out and place on wastebasket. Cover fits under top lip.

4. Make bow and attach with brass safety pin.

clothes hamper skirt

For easy access, the top of the hamper is not covered.

Supplies

Fabric	Piece	Amount
G	skirt	1¼ yards (1.2 meters)
½" (1.25 cm) wide elastic		1¼ yards (1.2 meters)
1½" (3.75 cm) wide wired-edge ribbon		1½ yards (1.4 meters)
Purchased plastic clothes hamper*		

*The hamper shown is 17" (42.5 cm) tall, with a top circumference of 58" (145 cm).

Cutting

Fabric	Piece	Cut	Size
G	skirt	3	20" × 40" (50 cm × 100 cm)
Elastic		1	40" (100 cm)

instructions

1. Place skirt pieces right sides together, with raw edges matching. Using ½" (1.25 cm) seam allowance, stitch together each 20" (50 cm) end. Press seams open (fig. 1-55).

2. Turn up top and bottom edges ½" (1.25 cm), then 1" (2.5 cm), to make double-fold hems. Press and stitch in place, leaving a 2" (5 cm) opening in the top edge to insert elastic (fig. 1-56).

3. Insert elastic in top casing. Stitch ends of elastic together, trimming any excess length. Stitch opening closed. Turn right side out and place on hamper. Skirt will fit under top lip.

4. Make bow and attach with brass safety pin.

•measuring for clothes hamper skirt and wastebasket cover•

Measure the height. Measure the circumference of the top and bottom. Prepare a strip of fabric with a length equal to twice the top circumference and a width equal to the height plus 3" (7.5 cm). The elastic length is approximately three-fourths the circumference measurement. Skirt and cover are finished in the same way, except skirt uses elastic in top casing only.

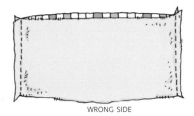

WRONG SIDE

fig. 1-55

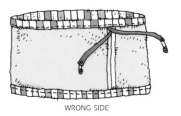

WRONG SIDE

fig. 1-56

Home from the Hospital
Baby's Layette

2

Newborn babies need lots of sleepwear, soft and washable and easy to care for. And like Baby, these layette outfits can be special and beautiful. Dress Baby in the sacque set, then add booties, bonnet, and tiny mittens for a charming coming-home outfit. For warmth and protection from drafts both indoors and out, swaddle Baby in the receiving blanket and quilted flannel throw.

fabric suggestions

These projects work up well in flannel, cotton, batiste, cotton double-knit, cotton/polyester blend, or cotton/polyester double-knit fabrics.

long kimono jacket

* *

This charming kimono jacket is perfect for newborns. The pattern is also the basis for the short kimono jacket on page 23 and the nightgown in Chapter 4.

Supplies

Fabric	Amount
A	1 yard (1 meter)
Narrow double-fold bias tape	1/3 yard (0.3 meter)
1/4" (0.75 cm) wide double-faced satin ribbon	1 1/4 yards (1.2 meters)

Cutting

The patterns are provided, beginning on page 115. Using a photocopier, enlarge as directed. Follow the cutting instructions on the patterns.

instructions

Use ½″ (1.25 cm) seam allowance unless noted otherwise.

1. Turn up each sleeve hem ¼″ (0.75 cm), then ½″ (1.25 cm), forming a double-fold hem. Press and stitch in place (fig. 2-1).

2. With right sides together and pattern symbols matching, pin sleeves to fronts and back. Stitch in place (fig. 2-2).

3. With right sides together, pin fronts and back together at sides and sleeves. Stitch in place (fig. 2-3).

4. Turn under the center front edges ¼″ (0.75 cm), then ½″ (1.25 cm), forming a double-fold hem (fig. 2-4). Press and stitch in place. Repeat for bottom edge of kimono; to miter corners, turn down corner points at 45° angle (fig. 2-5).

5. Place bias tape over neck edge with narrower side of bias on top. Pin, then stitch in place from front. Fold under ends for a neat finish (fig. 2-6).

6. Cut four pieces of ribbon, each about 11″ (27.5 cm) long. Fold over end of each ribbon length to make a small loop. Pin in position, then stitch to hold. Ribbons are sewn at neck edge and 4″ (10 cm) down along kimono fronts (fig. 2-7).

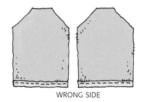

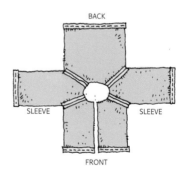

WRONG SIDE

fig. 2-1

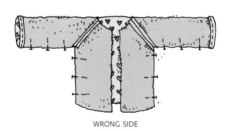

BACK

SLEEVE   SLEEVE

FRONT

fig. 2-2

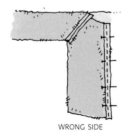

WRONG SIDE

fig. 2-3

WRONG SIDE

fig. 2-4

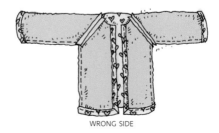

WRONG SIDE

fig. 2-5

fig. 2-6

RIGHT SIDE

fig. 2-7

sacque set

This easy-to-make sacque set makes a lovely gift for the new baby in your life.

short kimono jacket

•tip•

The same pattern is used to make the short kimono jacket, the long kimono jacket (page 21), and the nightgown (page 50). Save time by using production sewing methods. Cut out all three, then assemble in stages, i.e., all arm seams, all side seams, all neck edges, etc. It's much quicker to make several at once rather than one at a time.

Supplies

Fabric	Amount
A	¾ yard (0.75 meter)
Narrow double-fold bias tape	⅓ yard (0.3 meter)
¼″ (0.75 cm) wide double-faced satin ribbon	1¼ yards (1.2 meters)

Cutting

The patterns are provided, beginning on page 115. Using a photocopier, enlarge as directed. Follow the cutting instructions on the patterns.

instructions

Use ½″ (1.25 cm) seam allowance unless noted otherwise.

1. Follow instructions for long kimono jacket, Steps 1–3.

2. Starting at top of one front, turn under ¼″ (0.75 cm), then ½″ (1.25 cm), forming a double-fold hem. Continue around edge to top of other front. Press and stitch in place (fig. 2-8).

3. Follow instructions for long kimono jacket, Steps 5 and 6.

fig. 2-8

• •

Supplies

Fabric	Amount
A	½ yard (0.5 meter)
½" (1.25 cm) wide elastic for waist	½–¾ yard (0.5–0.75 meter)
¼" (0.75 cm) wide elastic for legs	½–¾ yard (0.5–0.75 meter)

Cutting

The patterns are provided, beginning on page 115. Using a photocopier, enlarge as directed. Follow the cutting instructions on the pattern.

instructions

Use ½" (1.25 cm) seam allowance unless noted otherwise.

1. With right sides together, pin front to back, matching center front and center back seams. Stitch (fig. 2-9).

2. Matching center seams, pin front to back at crotch seam. Stitch (fig. 2-10).

3. For each leg opening, make casing for elastic by folding over edge ¼" (0.75 cm), then ½" (1.25 cm). Stitch at top of fold, leaving 2" (5 cm) opening to insert elastic. Make casing for elastic at waist by folding over edge ¼" (0.75 cm), then ¾" (2 cm). Stitch as for leg openings.

4. Measure baby's upper thigh and waist. Cut elastic to that size plus 1" (2.5 cm). Insert elastic into casings; stitch ends together. Slipstitch casing opening closed (fig. 2-11).

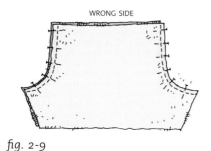

fig. 2-9

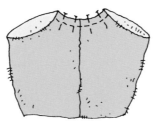

fig. 2-10

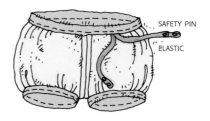

fig. 2-11

baby bonnet

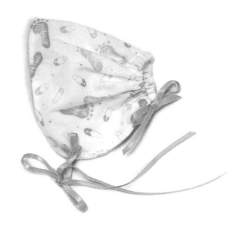

This bonnet is so much fun to sew, you'll want to make several for Baby.

Supplies

Fabric	Amount
Fabric scrap	6½″ × 14″ (16.25 cm × 35 cm)
¼″ (0.75 cm) wide double-faced satin ribbon	1¾ yards (1.6 meters)

Cutting

Fabric	Piece	Cut	Size
Fabric scrap	bonnet	1	6½″ × 14″ (16.25 cm × 35 cm)
Ribbon	bonnet back tie	1	17″ (42.5 cm)
	chin ties	2	20″ (50 cm)

•how to measure for a bonnet•

Measure from earlobe to earlobe across the top of the head, then adjust length as needed. Average head size is about 14″ (35 cm).

instructions

1. Round off corners on each end of one long side (fig. 2-12).

2. Overcast curved edge, then turn up ¼″ (0.75 cm). Press and topstitch to hem (fig. 2-13).

3. Make casing along remaining long edge by turning up ¼″ (0.75 cm), then ½″ (1.25 cm). Press and stitch along top edge of fold (fig. 2-14).

4. Thread 17″ (42.5 cm) ribbon through casing. Pull ribbon to gather bonnet back, and tie bow to form back of bonnet. Adjust to fit by tying ribbon to make back opening larger or smaller (fig. 2-15).

5. Fold over end of a 20″ (50 cm) ribbon to make three loops. Stitch in place for chin tie. Repeat for second tie.

fig. 2-12

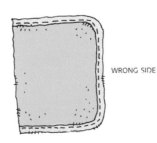

fig. 2-13

WRONG SIDE

fig. 2-14

fig. 2-15

baby booties and sleep mitts

Keep tiny toes and fingers warm with these sweet little booties and mitts.

Supplies

Fabric	Amount
A	¼ yard (0.25 meter)
¼" (0.75 cm) wide double-faced satin ribbon	½ yard (0.5 meter)

Cutting

The patterns are provided beginning on page 115. Using a photocopier, enlarge as directed. Follow the cutting instructions on the patterns.

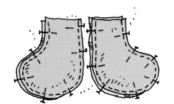

fig. 2-16

instructions

1. With right sides together, pin left side of bootie to right side. Using ¼" (0.75 cm) seam, stitch center bootie seam by sewing around edge, leaving top open. Repeat for second bootie (fig. 2-16).

2. Turn right side out. Make double-fold hem inside bootie by folding in top edge ¼" (0.75 cm), then 1¾" (4.5 cm). Press hem and stitch in place (fig. 2-17).

3. To make a casing, stitch ½" (1.25 cm) from first seam (fig. 2-18).

4. Unpick outside center seam between casing lines. Cut ribbon into two 9" (22.5 cm) pieces. Thread one ribbon through casing.

5. Repeat Steps 2–4 for second bootie.

6. Using pattern for sleep mitts, repeat Steps 1–4.

fig. 2-17

fig. 2-18

bib

• •

Make this bib to protect Baby's new clothes.

Supplies

Fabric	Amount
Flannel scrap	9″ × 10″ (22.5 cm × 25 cm)
Terrycloth scrap	9″ × 10″ (22.5 cm × 25 cm)
Narrow double-fold bias tape	1 yard (1 meter)

Cutting

The patterns are provided, beginning on page 115. Using a photocopier, enlarge as directed. Follow the cutting instructions on the pattern.

instructions

1. Pin bib pieces right sides together. Using a ¼″ (0.75 cm) seam allowance, sew around outside edge, leaving neck open (fig. 2-19).

2. Turn right side out. Topstitch ⅜″ (1 cm) from outside edge (fig. 2-20).

3. Starting with center point of bias tape at center of neck, pin tape over neck edge. Stitch neck edge first, then continue stitching along length of bias tape (fig. 2-21).

> **•option•**
>
> For a personal touch, appliqué a design or embroider Baby's name on the bib.

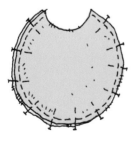

fig. 2-19

fig. 2-20

fig. 2-21

receiving blanket

Babies love to be swaddled in a cozy receiving blanket.

Supplies

Fabric	Piece	Amount
A	top	1 yard (1 meter)
B	back	1 yard (1 meter)

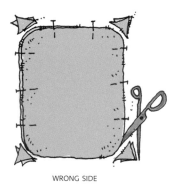

WRONG SIDE

fig. 2-22

Cutting

Fabric	Piece	Cut	Size
A	top	1	36″ × 36″ (90 cm × 90 cm)
B	back	1	36″ × 36″ (90 cm × 90 cm)

instructions

1. Pin squares with right sides together. Round off corners (fig. 2-22).

2. Stitch around outside edge, leaving small opening for turning (fig. 2-23).

3. Turn right side out. Slipstitch opening closed. Topstitch around outside, ⅜″ (1 cm) from edge (fig. 2-24). If desired, topstitch using decorative machine stitch.

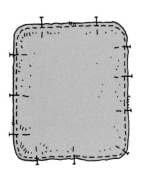

WRONG SIDE

fig. 2-23

RIGHT SIDE

fig. 2-24

quilted flannel throw

Make an "instant" blanket using prequilted fabric. Cut to size, bind the edges, and it's finished.

Supplies

Fabric	Amount
Prequilted double-faced flannel	1½ yards (1.4 meters)
Extra-wide double-fold bias tape	5½ yards (5.1 meters)

instructions

1. Square up fabric as needed. Round off corners (fig. 2-25).

2. Slip bias tape over raw edge of fabric, pinning carefully. Where end of bias overlaps, turn under for a neat finish. Stitch in place (fig. 2-26).

fig. 2-25

fig. 2-26

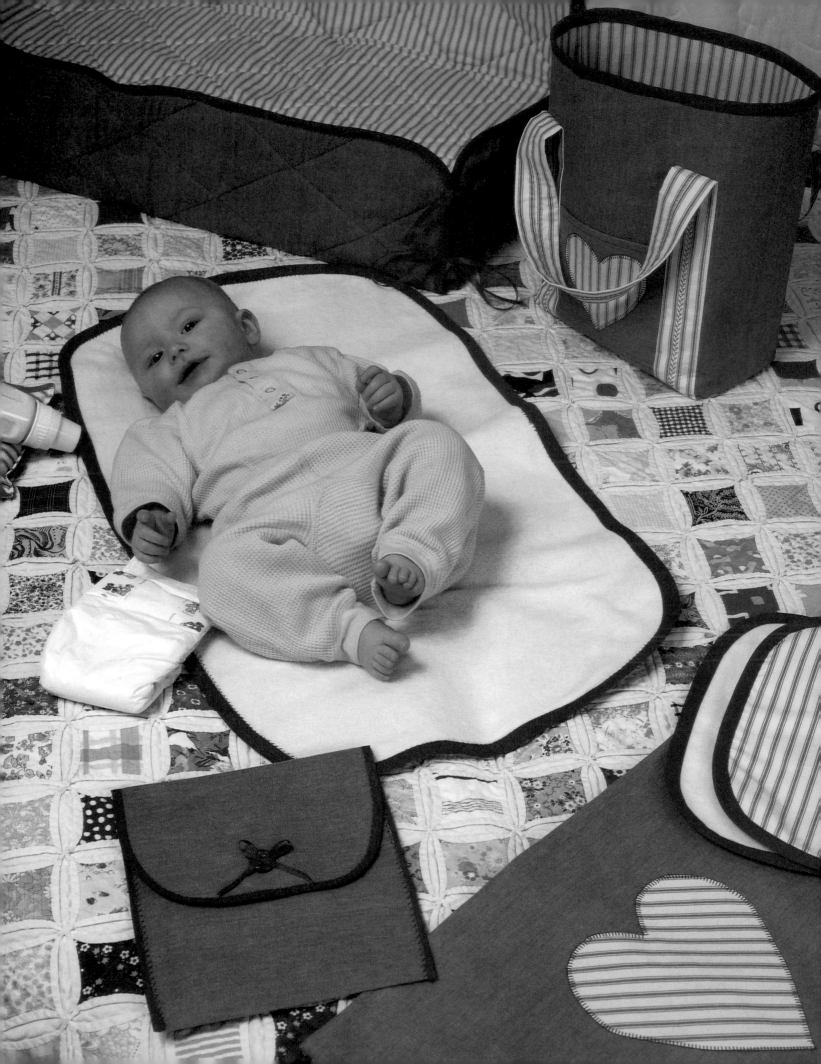

Baby on the Go
Practical Portables

3

When you visit friends and relatives, you'll want to have necessities like diapers and extra bottles close at hand. Here are practical items that make it easy to care for baby away from home.

fabric suggestions

These projects work up well in denim, ticking, duck, canvas, terrycloth, or decorator fabrics. The projects shown use three coordinating fabrics.

When using fusibles, remember to follow manufacturer's directions carefully. Otherwise, you may scorch the fabric or end up with a sticky mess on your iron and ironing board.

•tip•

When using fusibles, remember to follow manufacturer's directions carefully. Otherwise, you may scorch the fabric or end up with a sticky mess on your iron and ironing board.

Cut fusibles ½" (1.25 cm) smaller than fabric so that they won't stick to the ironing board. Or, iron the fusibles onto a larger piece of fabric, then cut to desired size.

diaper tote

● ●

This tote bag is perfect for keeping spare diapers and other necessities with you at all times. The straps go around and under the bottom for reinforcement.

Supplies

Fabric	Piece	Amount
A	tote and pockets	½ yard (0.5 meter)
B	tote lining, straps, and heart	¾ yard (0.75 meter)
Fusible interfacing		1¼ yards (1.2 meters)
Fusible vinyl		1 yard (1 meter)
Paper-backed fusible web		5″ × 10″ (12.5 cm × 25 cm)
Extra-wide double-fold bias binding		1 yard (1 meter)

Cutting

The patterns are provided, beginning on page 115. Using a photocopier, enlarge as directed. Follow the cutting instructions on the pattern.

Fabric	Piece	Cut	Size
A	tote	2	15″ × 15″ (37.5 cm × 37.5 cm)
	pockets	2	7″ × 11″ (17.5 cm × 27.5 cm)
B	tote lining	2	15″ × 15″ (37.5 cm × 37.5 cm)
	straps	2	4½″ × 42″ (11.25 cm × 105 cm)
	heart appliqué	2	5″ × 5″ (12.5 cm × 12.5 cm)
Fusible vinyl		2	14½″ × 14½″ (36.25 cm × 36.25 cm)
Fusible interfacing		2	14½″ × 14½″ (36.25 cm × 36.25 cm)
Fusible interfacing		2	4″ × 42″ (10 cm × 105 cm)

fig. 3-1

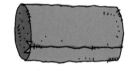

fig. 3-2

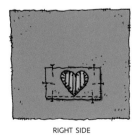

RIGHT SIDE

fig. 3-3

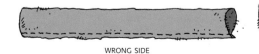

WRONG SIDE

fig. 3-4

RIGHT SIDE—FRONT OF STRAP

fig. 3-5

instructions

1. Fuse interfacing to wrong side of tote pieces and strap pieces.

2. Fold pocket piece in half lengthwise. Sew ½" (1.25 cm) seam, and finger press seam open. Turn right side out. Iron pocket flat so that seam is 1" (2.5 cm) from bottom edge (fig. 3-1).

3. Trace heart pattern onto paper side of fusible web. Iron fusible web to wrong side of appliqué fabric. Cut out heart. Center heart on pocket front and fuse in position. Using machine blanket stitch, sew around edges of heart, catching all fabric layers. Topstitch across top of pocket ¼" (0.75 cm) from edge (fig. 3-2).

4. Pin pocket on tote, 3½" (8.75 cm) from bottom and centered between side edges. Stitch along bottom of pocket, 1/16" (0.25 cm) from edge (fig. 3-3). Repeat Steps 2–4 for second pocket.

5. Fold strap piece in half lengthwise, right sides together, and stitch along long edge with ¼" (0.75 cm) seam allowance (fig. 3-4).

6. Turn right side out. Press with seam centered on back side.

7. On front of strap, sew decorative machine stitch down middle, sewing through all layers (fig. 3-5). Repeat Steps 5–7 for second strap. Change to a jeans needle (size 16/100) for Steps 8–10.

8. Position strap on tote front, overlapping sides of pocket as shown; pin in position. Starting at bottom edge, topstitch as close as possible to edge of strap, stopping 3" (7.5 cm) from top. Then stitch across and down other edge (fig. 3-6). Repeat Steps 4–7 for second strap.

9. Pin bag pieces together, right sides facing, matching straps at bottom. Using ½" (1.25 cm) seam allowance, sew sides and bottom. For added reinforcement, backstitch across straps in bottom seam (fig. 3-7).

10. To make box corner, fold bottom corner, matching side and bottom seams. This will make a point at end of bottom seam. Sew across end 2¼" (5.75 cm) from point. Trim point, leaving ½" (1.25 cm) seam allowance. Repeat on other corner (fig. 3-8). Press side seams open. Turn right side out.

11. Fuse iron-on vinyl to lining pieces. Using ⅝" (1.75 cm) seam allowance, sew together as for tote (Steps 9 and 10), but omit straps and leave right side to inside (fig. 3-9).

12. Pin lining in tote, matching side seams and top edges. Pin bias tape across top edges, easing tote and lining to fit if necessary. Overlap bias tape where ends meet, folding under top layer for a neat finish. Stitch through all layers (fig. 3-10).

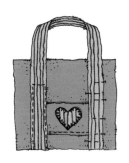

fig. 3-6   fig. 3-7

WRONG SIDE

2¼"

fig. 3-8   fig. 3-9

WRONG SIDE

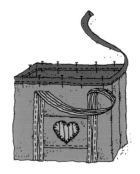

fig. 3-10

travel sleep mat and case

Baby always has a clean place for napping when Mother takes this sleep mat along. The sides fold up to keep drafts off Baby's face.

sleep mat

Supplies

Fabric	Piece	Amount
A	top	1 yard (1 meter)
B	bottom	1 yard (1 meter)
Extra-wide double-fold bias tape		4½ yards (4.2 meters)
Fusible fleece		1½ yards (1.4 meters)
¼" (0.75 cm) double-faced satin ribbon		5½ yards (5.1 meters)

Cutting

Fabric	Piece	Cut	Size
A	top	1	34" × 44" (85 cm × 110 cm)
B	bottom	1	34" × 44" (85 cm × 110 cm)
Ribbons		16	12" (30 cm)

fig. 3-11

MAT TOP
FLEECE MAT BOTTOM

fig. 3-12

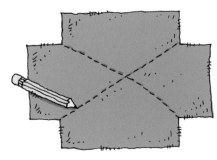

fig. 3-13

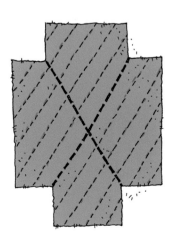

fig. 3-14

instructions

1. Cut a 7″ (17.5 cm) square out of each corner of mat top (fig. 3-11). Repeat for mat bottom.

2. Following manufacturer's directions, fuse batting to wrong side of mat bottom. Trim to same size.

3. Layer mat top, right side up, on top of fleece mat bottom. Pin-baste with brass safety pins to hold layers in position (fig. 3-12).

4. Draw a line diagonally across mat. Stitch along this line through all layers (fig. 3-13).

5. Stitch lines parallel to the first line, 4″ (10 cm) apart. Continue in this manner across mat (fig. 3-14).

6. Continue as in Step 5, stitching parallel lines 4″ (10 cm) apart (fig. 3-15).

7. Round off outside corners. Pin ribbons 2″ (5 cm) and 5″ (12.5 cm) away from inside corners (fig. 3-16).

8. Pin bias tape over raw edges, catching ribbon ends. Where end of bias tape overlaps beginning, fold under end for a neat finish, then stitch in place. To stitch along inside corners, simply pull corner open, forming a straightened edge (fig. 3-17).

9. To make the mat into a bed, pull up corners and tie.

•option•

Make the mat using double-sided prequilted fabric. Purchase 1 yard (1 meter) and cut 34″ × 44″ (85 cm × 110 cm). Follow Step 1, then Steps 8–10.

•tip•

To make the sleep mat water-resistant (and stiffer), fuse iron-on vinyl to the wrong side of the mat top.

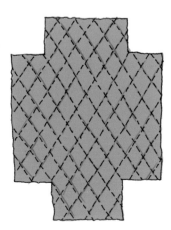

fig. 3-15

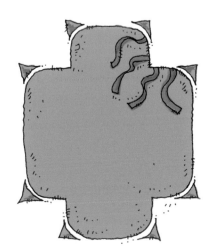

fig. 3-16

fig. 3-17

travel sleep mat case

· ·

When folded into its case, the sleep mat makes a soft travel pillow for toddlers.

Supplies

Fabric	Piece	Amount
A	case	½ yard (0.5 meter)
B	appliqué	7″ × 7″ (17.5 cm × 17.5 cm)

Cutting

The patterns are provided, beginning on page 115. Using a photocopier, enlarge as directed. Follow the cutting instructions on the pattern.

Fabric	Piece	Cut	Size
A	case	1	14″ × 41″ (35 cm × 102.5 cm)

instructions

1. Trace heart pattern onto paper backing of fusible web; then iron fusible web to wrong side of appliqué fabric. Cut out appliqué. Center on right side of case; fuse in position. Sew around heart with machine blanket stitch or satin stitch (fig. 3-19).

2. Make a double-fold hem on each short edge by turning up ¼″ (0.75 cm), then ½″ (1.25 cm). Press and stitch in place.

3. On wrong side, mark a foldline 10¾″ (27 cm) from each end (fig. 3-20).

4. Place wrong side down. Fold ends toward middle, overlapping about 3½″ (8.75 cm). Stitch across top and bottom (fig. 3-21).

5. Turn right side out; press. Fold the sleep mat to fit into the case.

RIGHT SIDE

fig. 3-19

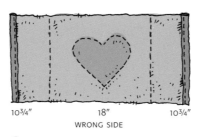

10¾″   18″   10¾″

WRONG SIDE

fig. 3-20

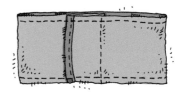

fig. 3-21

changing pad

Tuck this changing pad in your tote bag, so you will always have a clean surface available when changing Baby's diapers.

•tip•

For a decorative finish, sew along the edge of the bias tape with a machine feather stitch.

Supplies

Fabric	Piece	Amount
French terrycloth	top	½ yard (0.5 meter)
A	bottom	½ yard (0.5 meter)
Fusible vinyl		1 yard (1 meter)
Extra-wide double-fold bias tape		2¾ yards (2.6 meters)

Cutting

Fabric	Piece	Cut	Size
French terrycloth	top	1	18″ × 30″ (45 cm × 75 cm)
A	bottom	1	18″ × 30″ (45 cm × 75 cm)
Fusible vinyl		1	17½″ × 29½″ (43.75 cm × 73.75 cm)

instructions

1. Following manufacturer's directions, fuse vinyl to right side of bottom fabric (A) to make it moisture resistant. With wrong sides together, pin top to vinyl-backed bottom. Round off corners (fig. 3-22).

2. Stitch around edge, using ¼″ (0.75 cm) seam allowance.

3. Pin bias tape over raw edges, then stitch in place. Where end of bias tape overlaps beginning, fold under for a neat finish. Stitch through all layers (fig. 3-23).

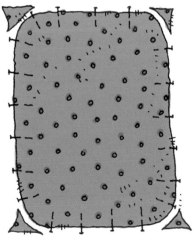

fig. 3-22

fig. 3-23

bottle holder

This holder is simply a bean bag with an elastic loop. It helps prop the bottle for Baby.

Supplies

Fabric	Amount
A	8″ × 8″ (20 cm × 20 cm)
B	8″ × 8″ (20 cm × 20 cm)

¼″ (0.75 cm) wide elastic   ¼ yard (0.25 meter)

2 sandwich-size plastic bags with zipper closure

1 pound of dried lentils or rice

instructions

1. Cut fabrics A and B from corner to corner into fourths (fig. 3-32).

2. Rearrange pieces as shown. Join with ¼″ (0.75 cm) seams to make two pieced blocks (fig. 3-33).

3. Make a ring with 7″ (17.5 cm) length of elastic, overlapping ends. Stitch by machine to center of one block (fig. 3-34).

4. With right sides together and elastic between layers, pin one block to the other. Using ¼″ (0.75 cm) seam allowance, stitch around edges twice, leaving a 4″ (10 cm) opening for turning and stuffing (fig. 3-35). Turn right side out.

5. To give the bottle holder weight and stability, lightly fill a sandwich-size plastic bag with dried beans or other legumes. Carefully seal bag closed; double-bag for extra security (fig. 3-36).

6. Insert bag of beans into holder. Carefully close opening using ladder stitch. Topstitch ⅛″ (0.5 cm) from outside edge (fig. 3-37). Extra stitching and double-bagging (Steps 4–6) is to keep beans away from Baby's prying fingers.

7. Slip bottle through elastic ring.

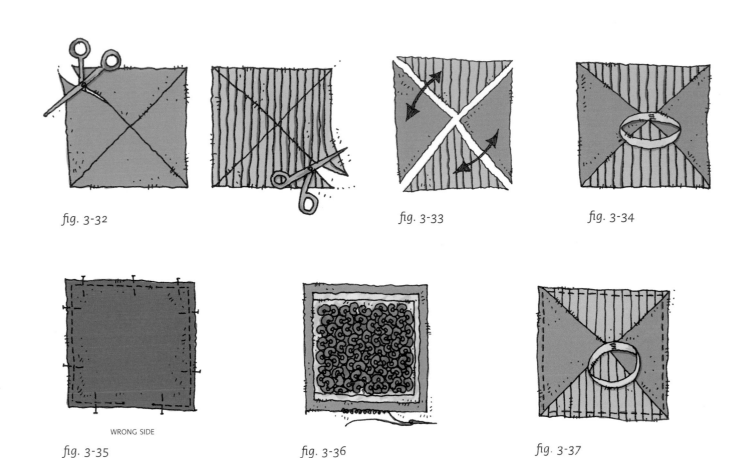

fig. 3-32

fig. 3-33

fig. 3-34

fig. 3-35

WRONG SIDE

fig. 3-36

fig. 3-37

Splish, Splash, Baby's in the Bath
Bath Time Essentials

4

Baby loves warm water and gentle splashes in the tub. These lovely bath linens, robe, and nightgown are easy to make. Put them in a lined toiletry basket for a thoughtful shower gift for a new mother.

fabric suggestions

Use French terrycloth for the bath linens. Use flannel, cotton, batiste, cotton double-knit, cotton/polyester blend, or cotton/polyester double-knit for the nightgown.

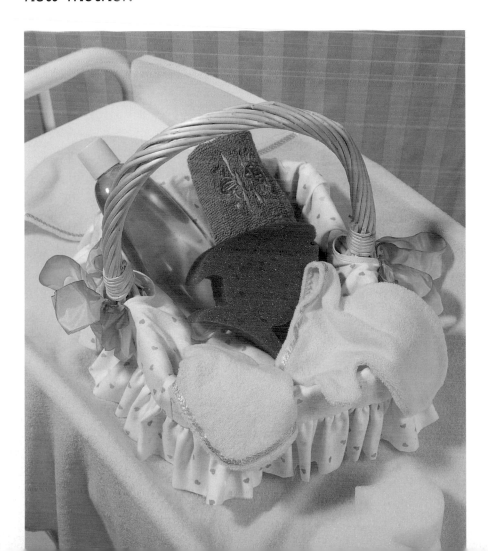

lined toiletry basket

A basket with a ruffled lining is practical for keeping baby toiletries organized, and it looks pretty, too.

Supplies

Fabric	Amount
Lining fabric*	
Narrow double-fold bias tape	½–¾ yard (0.5–0.75 meter)
Self-ruffle or purchased ruffle eyelet	
¼" (0.75 cm) wide double-faced satin ribbon	3 yards (2.75 meters)
Rectangular basket with handle	

*See Step 1 to calculate size.

instructions

1. Measure outside of basket from edge to edge to determine length and width. Add 1" (2.5 cm) to each measurement. Cut rectangle this size for lining (fig. 4-1).

2. Measure depth of basket.

fig. 4-1

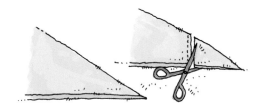

fig. 4-2

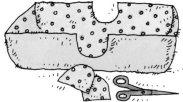

fig. 4-3

3. Fold one corner of lining on diagonal, matching one short edge of rectangle to adjacent long edge. Draw line where measurement from diagonal to straight edge equals basket depth. Stitch along line, then trim off corner (fig. 4-2).

4. Repeat for remaining three corners. Lining should fit loosely in basket and hang over top edge.

5. Cut a U-shaped notch to accommodate each handle. Notch should be approximately 2½″ (6.25 cm) deep and 2″ (5 cm) wide (fig. 4-3). Slip bias tape over raw edge of each notch; pin, then stitch in place.

6. Measure from notch to notch to determine length of self-ruffle or ruffled eyelet. (To make self-ruffle, see sidebar.)

7. With right sides together, pin ruffles to liner, one at each end, pinning from notch to notch. Stitch, then press ruffles away from liner (fig. 4-4).

8. Cut ribbon into four equal lengths. Make double loop at one end of ribbon, then stitch across ribbon loop to secure (fig. 4-5).

9. Stitch ribbon to one side of notch (fig. 4-6). Repeat for remaining ribbon lengths.

10. Place liner in basket. Tie ribbons into bows.

•how to make a self-ruffle for basket liner•

1. Cut a piece of fabric with a length equal to two and one-half times the distance from notch to notch, and a width of 6″ (15 cm). If you need a finished ruffle wider than 2½″ (6.25 cm), adjust width accordingly.

2. Fold fabric in half lengthwise. Press.

3. With right sides together, stitch ends to close. Turn right side out and press.

4. Using a long machine basting stitch, sew raw edges together. Sew a second line of stitching ⅜″ (1 cm) from first line and within seam allowance. Mark center point, then pull threads to gather fabric. Adjust the gathers. The ruffle is now ready to be sewn to basket liner (Step 7 left).

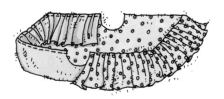

fig. 4-4

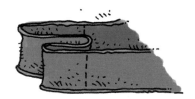

fig. 4-5

fig. 4-6

towel with hooded corner

This traditional baby bath towel is quick and easy to make. The corner hood is handy when bathing newborns.

Supplies

Fabric	Amount
French terrycloth	1 yard (1 meter)
¼″ (0.75 cm) wide double-faced satin ribbon	4¾ yards (4.4 meters)

Cutting

Patterns are provided, beginning on page 115. Using a photocopier, enlarge as directed. Follow the cutting instructions on the pattern.

Fabric	Piece	Cut	Size
French terrycloth	towel	1	36″ × 36″ (90 cm × 90 cm)

instructions

1. Overcast long edge of hood (fig. 4-7).

2. Turn under overcast edge approximately ⅜″ (1 cm), then pin ribbon along top edge. Use a decorative machine stitch, such as a feather stitch, to topstitch in place, catching the overcast edge and forming a hem. The ribbon will help stabilize stretchy terrycloth (fig. 4-8).

3. Pin hood to corner of towel, wrong sides up. Round off all corners. Stitch hood to corner using ⅜″ (1 cm) seam (fig. 4-9).

4. Overcast all edges of towel, then turn hood corner right side out. Starting at one hood edge and going around towel to other hood edge, turn under overcast edge ⅜″ (1 cm) and stitch ribbon in place as in Step 2 (fig. 4-10).

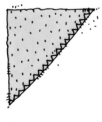

fig. 4-7

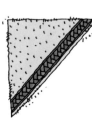

fig. 4-8

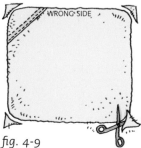

fig. 4-9

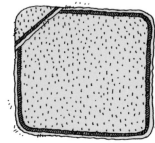

fig. 4-10

wash mitt

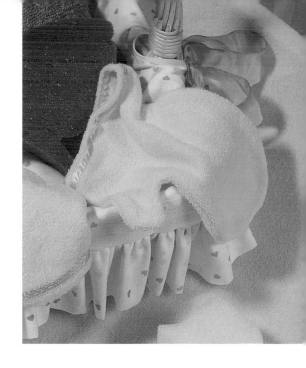

This wash mitt will fit most adult hands.

Supplies

Fabric	Amount
French terrycloth scrap	10" × 16" (25 cm × 40 cm)
¼" (0.75 cm) wide double-faced satin ribbon	½ yard (0.5 meter)

Cutting

Patterns are provided, beginning on page 115. Using a photocopier, enlarge as directed. Follow the cutting instructions on the pattern.

instructions

1. Cut out two mitt pieces. Overcast wrist edge on each (fig. 4-11).

2. With right sides together and using a ¼" (0.75 cm) seam allowance, stitch around outside edges, leaving bottom open for wrist (fig. 4-12).

3. Turn right side out. Fold under overcast wrist edge, then pin ribbon along outside edge. Use a decorative machine stitch to topstitch in place, catching overcast edge and forming a hem. Ribbon will help stabilize stretchy terrycloth (fig. 4-13).

•washcloth•

To make a washcloth, use a scrap of French terrycloth about 10" (25 cm) square. Round off the corners, overcast, and turn under edges. Use a decorative machine stitch to topstitch a ribbon along the edge. The ribbon will help stabilize the stretchy terrycloth.

fig. 4-11

WRONG SIDE

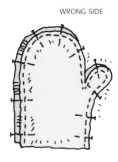

fig. 4-12

fig. 4-13

wraparound robe

. . . .

After bath is over, Baby stays warm in this delightful wraparound robe. This is a good beach item for toddlers, too.

Supplies

Fabric	Amount
60″ (150 cm) wide French terrycloth	1 yard (1 meter)
¼″ (0.75 cm) wide double-faced satin ribbon	6 yards (5.5 meters)

Cutting

Fabric	Piece	Cut	Size
French terrycloth	robe	1	26″ × 60″ (65 cm × 150 cm)
French terrycloth	hood	1	10″ × 20″ (25 cm × 50 cm)

fig. 4-14   fig. 4-15

instructions

1. Overcast one long edge of hood piece.

2. Turn under overcast edge approximately ⅜″ (1 cm), then pin ribbon along top edge. Use a decorative machine stitch, such as a feather stitch, to topstitch ribbon in place, catching the overcast edge and forming a hem. The ribbon will help stabilize stretchy terrycloth (fig. 4-14).

3. Fold the piece in half crosswise, right sides together, then round off one corner as shown. Stitch seam up back of hood. Overcast seam edge (fig. 4-15).

4. Round off corners on robe piece, then overcast all edges (fig. 4-16).

5. Mark center point on long side of robe piece. Match bottom of hood seam to this point, right sides together. Pin, then stitch using ¼″ (0.75 cm) seam allowance. Overcast edge (fig. 4-17).

6. Starting at edge of hood, fold under overcast edge of robe and topstitch ribbon in place as in Step 2 (fig. 4-18).

fig. 4-16

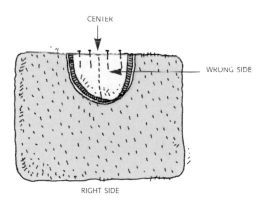

fig. 4-17

fig. 4-18

Out and About
Baby's First Outing

5

Fresh air and a daily walk keep Baby healthy. It's a relaxing break for Mother, too, especially when passersby smile at her beautiful baby. Make this delightful hooded jacket and bunting sack with matching pram coverlet, and Baby will be best-dressed in the park.

fabric suggestions

These projects work up well in polar fleece, pinwale corduroy, prequilted fabrics (nylon, flannel, cotton), or blanket wool (if lined with flannel).

jacket with hood and mittens
. . . .

Ears, of course, are optional. But with a cute puppy print like this, they are irresistible. Foldover mitts keep Baby's hands warm.

Supplies

Fabric	Amount
60" (150 cm) wide polyester fleece (A)	1 yard (1 meter)
Flannel scrap (C)	7" × 8" (17.5 cm × 20 cm)
Three ¾" (2 cm) diameter buttons	
3 Velcro dots or squares	
¼" (0.75 cm) cord for drawstring (optional)	1 yard (1 meter)

Cutting

The patterns are provided, beginning on page 115. Using a photocopier, enlarge as directed. Follow the cutting instructions on the patterns.

•tip•

Fleece doesn't ravel, but raw edges should be finished (see page III). Polar fleece is very fuzzy. Be sure to clean your bobbin case and/or serger often while sewing these projects.

instructions

Use 1/20 (1.25 cm) seam allowances unless noted otherwise.

1. Pin hood pieces right sides together. Sew along curved edge (fig. 5-1).

2. Hem front (face) edge by turning up edge ½″ (1.25 cm), then stitching in place (fig. 5-2).

3. Pin ear lining to ear, right sides together. Sew around ear, leaving top edge open. Repeat for second ear (fig. 5-3).

4. Turn ears right side out. Stuff lightly, if desired. Turn raw edges to inside and slipstitch closed, pulling threads to gather slightly. Use slipstitch to attach ears to hood, positioning each ear approximately 2½″ (6.25 cm) from the center seam (fig. 5-4).

5. Hem mitt by folding edge ½″ (1.25 cm) toward wrong side and top-stitching (fig. 5-5).

6. Pin mitt to sleeve back, right sides together. Stitch along side edge only (fig. 5-6).

7. Pin sleeve front to sleeve back, right sides together, matching pattern symbols. Stitch along top of sleeve only (fig. 5-7). Repeat Steps 5–7 for second sleeve.

•option•

If desired, add a drawstring to the hood. Insert a buttonhole or grommet where marked on the pattern. Do this before hemming the bottom edge (Step 13).

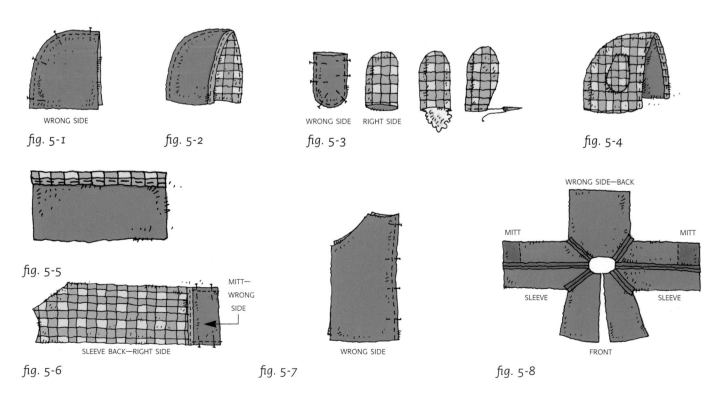

WRONG SIDE

fig. 5-1

fig. 5-2

WRONG SIDE   RIGHT SIDE

fig. 5-3

fig. 5-4

fig. 5-5

MITT—WRONG SIDE

SLEEVE BACK—RIGHT SIDE

fig. 5-6

WRONG SIDE

fig. 5-7

WRONG SIDE—BACK

MITT   MITT

SLEEVE   SLEEVE

FRONT

fig. 5-8

8. Pin sleeves to jacket back and jacket fronts, right sides together, matching symbols. Stitch seams. Staystitch neck edge (fig. 5-8).

9. Pin each side, right sides together, matching underarm seams. Sew, starting at wrist and ending at bottom edge (fig. 5-9).

10. Turn jacket right side out. Overcast sleeve edge, taking care to sew mitt to sleeve back (fig. 5-10). Fold edge ½″ (1.25 cm) to inside. Hem by hand with slipstitches.

11. Pin hood in position, matching hood seam to center back of jacket, then stitch (fig. 5-11).

12. Press seam away from hood and toward jacket. Topstitch next to hood seam, catching seam allowance in topstitching (fig. 5-12).

13. Hem front and bottom edges by turning under ¾″ (2 cm) and mitering corners. Stitch in place (fig. 5-13).

14. Sew Velcro at neck edge and at 1″ (2.5 cm) intervals down jacket front (fig. 5-13). Put softer loop on inside placket so that it won't irritate Baby's neck. Sew buttons on top of outside placket for decoration.

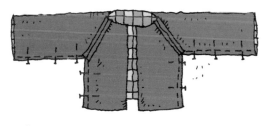

fig. 5-9

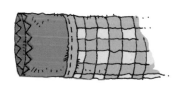

WRONG SIDE   RIGHT SIDE

fig. 5-10

fig. 5-11

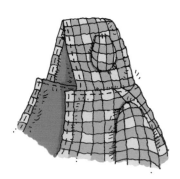

fig. 5-12

fig. 5-13

bunting sack

This bunting sack is big and comfy on newborns, with lots of room to kick and squirm.

Supplies

Fabric	Amount
60″ (150 cm) wide double-faced polyester fleece (B)	1 yard (1 meter)
1″ (2.5 cm) wide double-faced satin ribbon	1 yard (1 meter)

Cutting

Fabric	Piece	Cut	Size
Fleece	bunting sack	1	32″ × 42″ (80 cm × 105 cm)

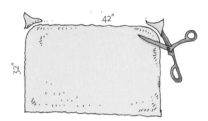

fig. 5-15

instructions

Use ½″ (1.25 cm) seam allowance unless noted otherwise.

1. Round off two corners on 42″ (105 cm) side, then overcast sides and top edges (fig. 5-15).

2. Fold in half crosswise, with right sides together and 32″ (80 cm) edges matching. Stitch from straight corners to 12″ (30 cm) below curved corners. Seam will be 20″ (50 cm) long (fig. 5-16).

3. With right sides together, refold to match center front seam to center back, then stitch across bottom (fig. 5-17).

4. To make a gusset, fold the bottom corner, matching side and bottom seams. This will make a point at the end of bottom seam. Sew across each end 3″ (7.5 cm) from point. Trim point, leaving ½″ (1.25 cm) seam allowance. Repeat on other corner (fig. 5-18).

5. Turn right side out. Fold top opening ½″ (1.25 cm) to inside. Top stitch.

6. If desired, add bow trim at bottom of front opening.

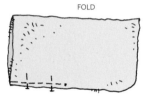

fig. 5-16

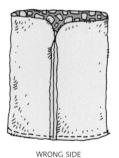

fig. 5-17

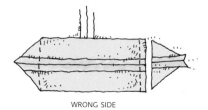

fig. 5-18

nine-patch pram coverlet

This is a good project to make from leftover fleece. It's easy and quick, especially with a serger.

Supplies

Fabric	Piece	Amount
60″ (150 cm) wide polyester fleece (A)	top	¾ yard (0.75 meter)
60″ (150 cm) wide polyester fleece (B)	top	¾ yard (0.75 meter)
45″ (112.5 cm) wide flannel (D)	back	1¼ yards (1.2 meters)

Cutting

Fabric	Piece	Cut	Size
A	top	5	12½″ × 12½″ (31.25 cm × 31.25 cm)
B	top	4	12½″ × 12½″ (31.25 cm × 31.25 cm)
D	back	1	36″ × 36″ (90 cm × 90 cm)

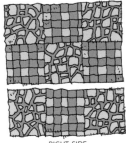

RIGHT SIDE

fig. 5-20

WRONG SIDE

fig. 5-21

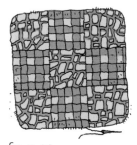

fig. 5-22

instructions

1. With right sides together and alternating fabrics, sew fleece squares together to make three rows. Sew rows together (fig. 5-20).

2. Pin pieced top to flannel backing, right sides together. The flannel is slightly bigger all around than fleece. However, because fleece is so stretchy, the excess will be taken up in Step 4. Round off corners (fig. 5-21).

3. Sew around all sides, leaving a 5″ (12.5 cm) opening for turning (fig. 5-22).

4. Turn right side out; hand stitch opening closed. Stitch-in-the-ditch to make tic-tac-toe lines, then stitch around outside, ½″ (1.25 cm) from edge (fig. 5-23).

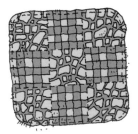

fig. 5-23

Playtime!
Noah's Ark Playroom

6

Decorate Baby's room with a colorful Noah's ark quilt and wallhanging. Easy-to-make stuffed animals can be stored in the ark after Baby is done playing with them. A mobile with felt animals and ark hangs above Baby's crib.

fabric suggestions

These projects work up well in cottons, cotton/polyester blends, decorator fabrics, or felt. The quilt shown uses 21 coordinating fabrics. The wallhanging and the stuffed animals each use six coordinating fabrics. The mobile uses four colors of felt.

noah's ark crib quilt

Use scraps from your stash to make this colorful quilt. Motifs are fused in place on the quilt top, then layers are assembled and quilted.

Supplies

Fabric	Piece	Amount
A	ocean	¾ yard (0.75 meter)
B	sky	¾ yard (0.75 meter)
C	borders	1¾ yards (1.6 meters)
D	center back	1¾ yards (1.6 meters)
E	outside back and Noah's coat	1¾ yards (1.6 meters)
F	ark roof	8″ × 17″ (20 cm × 42.5 cm)

noah's ark wallhanging

Each section of ark is made separately, then the sections are sewn together. The ark front and back form a pocket to hold animals. A hidden dowel rod on the back of the ark stabilizes the pocket.

Supplies

Fabric	Piece	Amount
L	ark house	½ yard (0.5 meter)
M	door	6″ × 7″ (15 cm × 17.5 cm)
X	windows	3″ × 6″ (7.5 cm × 15 cm)
V	ark roof and tabs	½ yard (0.5 meter)
A	ark bottom front	¾ yard (0.75 meter)
W	ark bottom back, ark pocket, rod pocket*	1¾ yards (1.6 meters)
Fusible batting		¾ yard (2.1 meters)
½″ (1.25 cm) diameter wooden dowel rod		35″ long (87.5 cm)
6″ (15 cm) diameter decorative wooden or brass curtain rod		36″ long (90 cm)
Paper-backed fusible web		12″ × 12″ (30 cm × 30 cm)

*These pieces will not show on the finished wallhanging.

Cutting

The patterns are provided beginning on page 115. Using a photocopier, enlarge as directed. Follow the cutting instructions on the patterns.

instructions

Make the Ark House

1. Following manufacturer's directions, iron paper-backed fusible web to wrong side of door and window fabrics. Pin patterns to right side of fabrics and cut. Peel off paper backing.

2. Position door and windows on house front, then fuse in place (fig. 6-7).

3. Trim batting so it is ¼″ (0.75 cm) smaller all around than house. Fuse batting lightly to wrong side of house front (fig. 6-8). Take care not to press hard when fusing the batting or it will flatten and lose loft.

4. Using contrasting thread, outline door and windows with hand or machine blanket stitch (fig. 6-9).

RIGHT SIDE

fig. 6-7

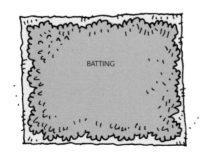

WRONG SIDE—HOUSE FRONT

fig. 6-8

5. Place house front on house back, right sides together (batting will be on bottom). Sew around all sides with ¼″ (0.75 cm) seam allowance, leaving an opening on bottom edge for turning (fig. 6-10). Clip corners and turn right side out, then close opening with ladder stitch.

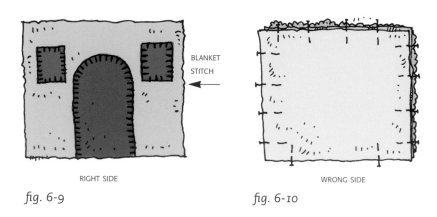

BLANKET STITCH

RIGHT SIDE

WRONG SIDE

fig. 6-9   fig. 6-10

Make the Ark Roof

6. Trim batting so it is ¼″ (0.75 cm) smaller all around than roof. Fuse batting to roof front (fig. 6-11).

7. Fold tab in half lengthwise, right sides facing. Stitch along raw edge to form a tube (fig. 6-12). Repeat to make three tabs.

8. Turn tabs right side out, centering seam on one side. Fold in half as shown, with seam to inside (fig. 6-13).

9. Pin tabs evenly along top of roof front, matching raw edges (fig. 6-14). Loops will point toward bottom of roof. Stitch in place.

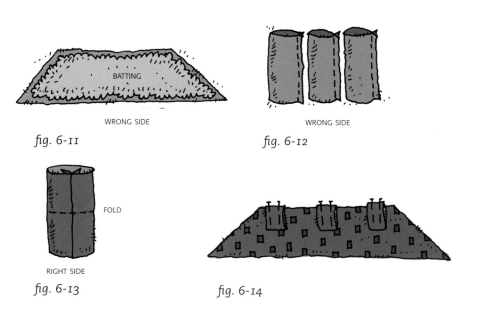

BATTING

WRONG SIDE

WRONG SIDE

fig. 6-11   fig. 6-12

FOLD

RIGHT SIDE

fig. 6-13   fig. 6-14

10. Place roof front on roof back, right sides together (batting will be on bottom and tabs will be between roof pieces). Sew around all sides with ¼″ (0.75 cm) seam allowance, leaving an opening on bottom edge for turning (fig. 6-15).

11. Clip corners and turn right side out, then close opening with ladder stitch. Machine quilt through all layers of roof (fig. 6-16).

•tips•

Quilting will make your roof look shingled. You can quilt just about any design as long it goes with the fabric. Try quilting randomly, following some of the design lines in the fabric.

Draw quilting lines with chalk or pencil, or quilt along lines in fabric.

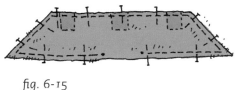

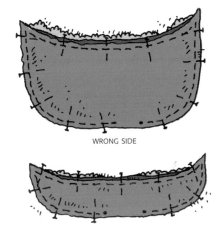

fig. 6-15   fig. 6-16

Make the Ark Bottom

12. Trim batting ¼″ (0.75 cm) smaller all around than ark bottom front and pocket front. Fuse to wrong side of both pieces (fig. 6-17).

13. Pin ark bottom front and back together, right sides facing (batting will be on bottom). Sew using ¼″ (0.75 cm) seam allowance, leaving a 6″ (15 cm) opening for turning. Repeat for pocket front and back (fig. 6-18).

14. Clip curves and corners, and turn right side out. Press, then close opening with ladder stitch. Quilt by hand or machine through all layers (fig. 6-19).

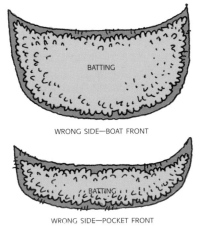

WRONG SIDE—BOAT FRONT

BATTING

WRONG SIDE—POCKET FRONT

BATTING

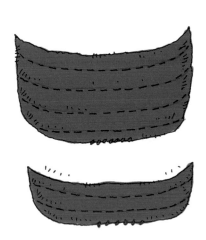

WRONG SIDE

fig. 6-17   fig. 6-18   fig. 6-19

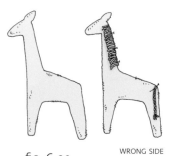

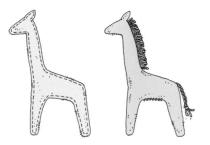

WRONG SIDE

fig. 6-32

fig. 6-33   fig. 6-34

specific instructions

Giraffe

1. Make tail 3½″ (8.75 cm) long. Make neck fringe 5″ (12.5 cm) long. Fold fringe in half along stitching line, then pin in position along neck of one body piece (fig. 6-32).

2. Place body pieces together, right sides facing. Tail and neck fringe will be hidden between layers. Stitch, leaving a small opening for turning (fig. 6-33).

   Tip: To make inside angles, square them off as you sew. Clip into corners. The angles will then turn right side out properly.

3. Clip curves, turn right side out, and stuff. Close opening (fig. 6-34).

Zebra

Make tail 3″ (7.5 cm) long. Make neck fringe 3″ (7.5 cm) long. Finish animal, following instructions for giraffe.

Whale

1. Make whale body, following general instructions. Turn right side out, stuff, and close opening.

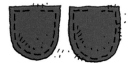

fig. 6-35

fig. 6-36

2. With right sides together, sew flippers, leaving an opening for turning. Clip curves and turn right side out. Stuff lightly (fig. 6-35).

3. Using heavy-duty thread and a ladder stitch, sew top edge of flippers onto body after whale is completed. Stitch each flipper twice to secure in place (fig. 6-36).

Elephant

1. Make elephant body, following general directions.

2. Make two ears as in whale flippers, Whale Step 2. Turn right side out. Stuff lightly; too much stuffing will make the ears look like wings.

3. Attach ears as for whale flippers, Whale Step 3. Embroider facial details, if desired, with hand or machine stitches. Or, use fabric pens with non-toxic permanent ink to outline features. Avoid using beads and other removable trims because Baby might pull off beads and swallow or choke on them.

Hippo

1. Make two ears and tail as for whale flippers, Whale Step 2. Clip curves and turn right side out. Pin ears and tail in place on right side of one hippo body.

2. With right sides together, stitch hippo body, leaving 2″ (5 cm) opening for turning. Ears and tail will be sandwiched between layers.

3. Finish, following general directions.

4. To make ears stand up, make a small tuck with hand stitches at base of ear back.

Lion

1. Make 3½″ (8.75 cm) tail. Make two pieces of fringe, 3″ (7.5 cm) and 12″ (30 cm) long, each 4″ (10 cm) wide. Pin 3″ (7.5 cm) fringe onto one body piece along head area as shown (fig. 6-41). Pin tail in position.

2. With right sides together, stitch around lion body, leaving a 2″ (5 cm) opening for turning. Fringe and tail will be sandwiched between body pieces. Turn right side out and stuff. Stitch opening closed.

3. Place head pieces together, right sides facing. Sew together with ¼″ (0.75 cm) seam allowance, but do NOT leave an opening for turning. Instead, cut opening in middle of head back piece for turning (fig. 6-42).

4. Turn head right side out and stuff. Seal edges of cut with fray-checking liquid, then whipstitch to close.

5. Fold 12″ (30 cm) length of fringe in half and pin in place around head, just behind head seamline and behind ears. Whipstitch in place, using fringe seam to anchor fringe (fig. 6-43). Secure thread (lock stitch) after each whipstitch (see Sewing Basics page 101).

6. Glue head onto body. When glue is dry, whipstitch head to body.

fig. 6-41   RIGHT SIDE

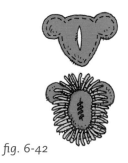

fig. 6-42

fig. 6-43

•how to make a tail•

Cut a piece of yarn at least 5′ (1.6 meters) long. Fold it in half, then thirds (fig. 6-37). Cut one end (fig. 6-38) and knot the other (fig.6-39). Braid, using two strands as one. Knot at desired length, leaving loose strands on the tail end (fig. 6-40). Sew the beginning knot into the seam.

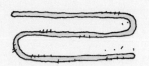

fig. 6-37

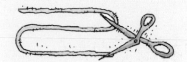

fig. 6-38

fig. 6-39

fig. 6-40

mobile

• •

Baby will be entertained by this simple mobile. Brightly colored felt animals surround Noah's ark and hang from wooden dowels glued into a baby block.

Supplies

Fabric	Amount
Felt in four colors	two 9″ × 12″ pieces each (two 22.5 cm × 30 cm pieces each)
Rattail cord in coordinating color	3 yards (2.75 meters)
Polyester stuffing	
Topstitching thread	
Size 16/100 (jeans) needle	
One wooden baby block	
Four ¼″ (0.75 cm) diameter, 9″ (22.5 cm) long wooden dowel rods	
Four wooden end caps for ¼″ (0.75 cm) dowels	
Two small brass eye hooks	
Wood glue	
Nontoxic acrylic paint to match felt	
Ceiling hook	

Cutting

The patterns are provided beginning on page 115. Using a photocopier, enlarge as directed. Follow the cutting instructions on the patterns.

fig. 6-44

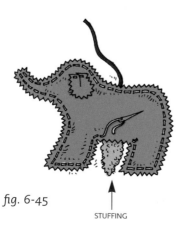

fig. 6-45

STUFFING

fig. 6-46

instructions

1. Cut animals with pinking shears. Knot one end of 10″ (25 cm) length of cord. Pin knot end of cord on wrong side of one animal shape, then pin tail and/or horn in position (fig. 6-44).

2. Place second shape on top, wrong sides together. Stitch by hand or machine, ⅜″ (1 cm) from all edges, leaving a small opening for stuffing. Stuff lightly and topstitch opening closed (fig. 6-45).

3. Pin ears in position, then attach securely with hand stitches. A pleat in the ear will make it stand up better. Attach flippers to whale with secure hand stitches.

4. Cut ark pieces with pinking shears. Sew door to house; then sew on roof and boat. Repeat for second ark.

5. Place one ark on top of another, wrong sides together. Pin 13″ (32.5 cm) knotted cord in position between layers. Stitch by hand or machine, ⅜″ (1 cm) from edge, leaving a small opening. Stuff lightly, then sew opening closed (fig. 6-46).

6. Paint dowel rods and end caps to match the animals.

7. Draw a chalk line from corner to corner to find center of each side of block (fig. 6-47).

8. Drill ⅜″ (1 cm) deep, ¼″ (0.75 cm) diameter hole on four sides. Put glue into holes, then insert dowel rod into each one. Put glue into each end cap, then put onto ends of rods (fig. 6-48). Put eye hook in top and bottom of block.

9. Attach cord to dowels using wrapped cord method (fig. 6-49). Wrap as shown, leaving the loop loose enough to be moved along dowel. Pull top thread to bring bottom end into center of wrap. Clip ends of wrapping cord. Balance is affected by weight of stuffing; slide cords along rods to balance mobile.

10. Measure distance from desired height of mobile to ceiling. Cut cord that length plus 2″ (5 cm). Attach to eye hook on top of block. Form loop to fit ceiling hook; wrap to secure. Attach mobile to ceiling, taking care to keep it out of Baby's reach.

fig. 6-47

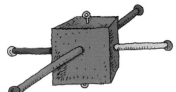

fig. 6-48

fig. 6-49

fig. 6-50

To Grandmother's House We Go

A Guest Room for Baby

7

When Baby is on the way, grandmothers want to prepare an extra bedroom for their grandchildren, but decorate it in colors that are suitable for adult guests, too. Here is a lovely crib quilt with matching throw pillows. When the crib is put away, the quilt will still make a lovely throw for the back of an armchair or folded at the foot of an adult-size bed. Grandmother's rocking chair has a padded armrest and cushions that coordinate with the quilt.

fabric suggestions

These projects work up well in broadcloth, cotton, calico, gingham, or decorator fabrics. The projects shown use five coordinating fabrics.

throw pillow with piped edge

Use extra fabric to make throw pillows. Piece the tops with squares or triangles, then finish with a piped or flanged edge.

Finished size is 16″ × 16″ (40 cm × 40 cm).

•pillow with flanged edge•

Piece pillow top as desired, then cut 21″ × 21″ (52.5 cm × 52.5 cm). Cut two backs, each 16″ × 21″ (40 cm × 52.5 cm). Finish as for pillow with piped edge. Turn right side out. To make flange, stitch 1½″ (3.75 cm) from outside edge. Insert 16″ (40 cm) pillow form. With flange, finished size will be 19″ × 19″ (47.5 cm × 47.5 cm).

•tip•

Use zipper foot when sewing on piping. Stitch as close to piping as possible. To join ends of piping, leave 2″ (5 cm) at beginning and end unstitched. Trim cord ½″ (1.25 cm) shorter than piping fabric. Overlap ends of piping and fold raw edges into seam. Stitch in place, then trim excess piping.

Supplies

Fabric	Piece	Amount
A	top	⅝ yard (0.6 meter)
B	top	⅝ yard (0.6 meter)
E	back	½ yard (0.5 meter)
¼″ (0.75) diameter cord for piping		2 yards (1.9 meters)
Extra-wide bias binding*		2 yards (1.9 meters)
16″ (40 cm) square pillow form		

*See Quilting Basics, page 107, if you wish to make your own binding from Fabric E.

Cutting

Fabric	Piece	Cut	Size
A	top	1	18¼″ × 18¼″ (45.75 cm × 45.75 cm)
B	top	1	18¼″ × 18¼″ (45.75 cm × 45.75 cm)
E	back	2	12″ × 17″ (30 cm × 42.5 cm)

instructions

1. Cut fabrics A and B on diagonals (fig. 7-8).

2. Rearrange pieces as shown. Using ¼″ (0.75 cm) seam, piece corners, then join along center diagonal (fig. 7-9).

3. On center edge of each back piece, turn up ¼″ (0.75 cm), then 1″ (2.5 cm), forming a double-fold hem. Press and stitch in place (fig. 7-10).

4. Place backs on top of front, right sides together. Backs will overlap in middle. Round off corners (fig. 7-11).

5. Make piping (see Sewing Basics, page 101). Starting in the middle of one side, pin piping to right side of pillow top, matching raw edges. Using zipper foot, machine stitch through all layers, overlapping ends as described in Tip (fig. 7-12).

6. Stack top and back pieces, right sides together, matching outside raw edges. Hemmed center back edges will overlap. Using ½″ (1.25 cm) seam allowance, stitch around outside edge immediately next to piping (fig. 7-13).

7. Trim excess seam allowance, clip curves, then turn right side out. Insert pillow form.

fig. 7-8

fig. 7-9

WRONG SIDE

WRONG SIDE

fig. 7-10

fig. 7-11

fig. 7-12

WRONG SIDE

fig. 7-13

rocking chair cushions

Make cushions to match the crib quilt. If you're using striped fabric, the stripes should run in the same direction on both cushions, even if the back and seat cushions are different sizes.

Supplies

Fabric	Piece	Amount
A	top and bottom*	1¾ yards (1.6 meters)
C	ruffle	1 yard (1 meter)
⅜" (1 cm) wide grosgrain ribbon		3½ yards (3.2 meters)

Two 15" × 17" × 2" (37.5 cm × 42.5 cm × 5 cm) polyurethane foam pads

*Includes fabric for two cushions.

Cutting

Fabric	Piece	Cut	Size
A	top	2	18" × 20" (45 cm × 50 cm)
	bottom	4	12" × 20" (30 cm × 50 cm)
C	ruffle	8	3½" × 44" (8.75 cm × 110 cm)*
Ribbon	ties	4	30" (75 cm)

*If using 54" (135 cm) wide fabric, cut six pieces, each one 3½" × 54" (8.75 cm × 135 cm).

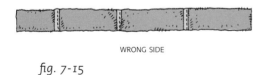

WRONG SIDE

fig. 7-14

WRONG SIDE

fig. 7-15

WRONG SIDE

fig. 7-16

instructions

1. On one long edge of each bottom piece, turn up ¼" (0.75 cm), then 1" (2.5 cm), forming a double-fold hem. Press hem carefully and stitch in place (fig. 7-14).

2. Using French seams (see Sewing Basics, page 101), sew four ruffle sections together along short sides, to make one long strip for each cushion (fig. 7-15).

3. Using rolled-edge foot (see Sewing Basics, page 101), hem one long edge of ruffle (fig. 7-16). Repeat for second ruffle.

4. Using French seam, join ends to make a circle. Sew gathering threads along raw edge (fig. 7-17).

5. Mark quarter points of ruffle and pillow top, then carefully pull threads and gather edge of ruffle.

   Tip: Gather each section separately, as in fig. 7-17. This will make your life easier if one of the gathering threads breaks.

6. With right sides together, pin ruffle to cushion top, matching quarter points. Spread gathers evenly between seams, allowing extra fullness at corners. To avoid seams at the cushion corners, position ruffle seams along the side edges of cushion. Position ribbon ties at corners, if desired. Stitch, using ⅜″ (1 cm) seam allowance. Backstitch over ribbon ties (fig. 7-18).

7. Stack top and bottom pieces, right sides together, matching outside raw edges. Hemmed center back edges will overlap; ruffle will be inside. Using ⅝″ (1.75 cm) seam allowance, stitch around outside edge (fig. 7-19). Turn right side out and insert foam pad. If more secure closure is desired, sew Velcro strips on overlap of back pieces (fig. 7-20).

8. Repeat Steps 5–7 for second cushion.

•tip•

When sewing on ruffle, gently round off corners with stitches. When turned right side out, the corners will look square and the ruffle will drape better

•tip•

Here's how to measure for seat cushion. Add 1″ (2.5 cm) to the length and width measurements of the cushion. If length/width measurements are different for chair seat and seat back, take care to allow for extra fabric so you can make stripes go the way you want.

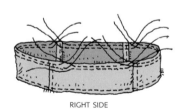

RIGHT SIDE

fig. 7-17

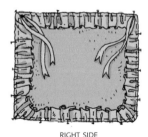

RIGHT SIDE

fig. 7-18

WRONG SIDE

fig. 7-19

RIGHT SIDE

fig. 7-20

rocking chair organizer

Organizer pockets hang from the armrest so you can keep baby accessories within reach.

Supplies

Fabric	Piece	Amount
A	top	½ yard (0.5 meter)
B	bottom	½ yard (0.5 meter)
C	pockets	½ yard (0.5 meter)
Extra-wide bias binding*		2½ yards (2.3 meters)
⅜″ (1 cm) wide grosgrain ribbon		1½ yards (1.4 meters)
Polyester fiber stuffing		

*See Quilting Basics page 107, if you wish to make your own binding.

Cutting

Fabric	Piece	Cut	Size
A	top	1	13″ × 24″ (32.5 cm × 60 cm)
B	bottom	1	13″ × 24″ (32.5 cm × 60 cm)
C	pocket 1	1	9″ × 13″ (22.5 cm × 32.5 cm)
	pocket 2	1	13″ × 14″ (32.5 cm × 35 cm)
Ribbon	ties	2	24″ (60 cm)

instructions

1. Fold Pocket 1 in half lengthwise; fold Pocket 2 in half crosswise. Press (fig. 7-21).

2. Stack top and bottom pieces, wrong sides together. Stitch a horizontal line through both layers, 7″ (17.5 cm) from one end. Stitch a second line 12″ (30 cm) from the other end (fig. 7-22).

3. Place pockets at ends with folds toward middle. Stitch from fold to edge, dividing each pocket as shown (fig. 7-23).

4. Round off corners. Using ¼″ (0.75 cm) seam allowance, stitch around outside edge, leaving a 5″ (12.5 cm) opening between center stitching lines on one edge (fig. 7-24).

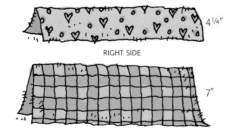

4¼″

RIGHT SIDE

7″

fig. 7-21

5. Stuff lightly through opening to form armrest. Do not overstuff, as it will be difficult to attach binding (fig. 7-25). Stitch opening closed.

6. On back, pin one ribbon tie at each end of stuffed section. Starting on one side, pin bias binding to front, right sides together, matching the edges. For a neat finish, fold over beginning of bias; overlap end. Then fold bias over edge to back side; use invisible hem stitch to secure (fig. 7-26).

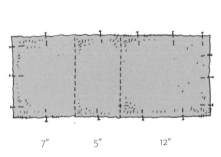

7"   5"   12"

fig. 7-22

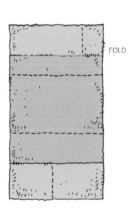

FOLD

fig. 7-23

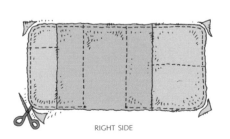

RIGHT SIDE

fig. 7-24

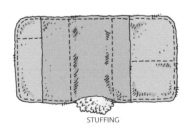

STUFFING

fig. 7-25

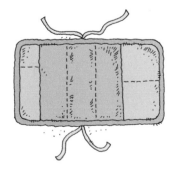

fig. 7-26

changing pad with cover

Make a changing pad with a moisture-resistant cover. If a dresser top is used as a changing table, be sure to put a nonskid mat under the pad.

Supplies

Fabric	Piece	Amount
B	top and bottom	1 yard (1 meter)
Fusible vinyl		½ yard (0.5 meter)

15″ × 31″ × 2″ (37.5 cm × 77.5 cm × 5 cm) foam pad

13″ × 31″ (32.5 cm × 77.5 cm) nonskid carpet mat

Cutting

Fabric	Piece	Cut	Size
B	top	1	15″ × 31″ (37.5 cm × 77.5 cm)
	bottom	2	15″ × 20½″ (37.5 cm × 51.25 cm)
Fusible vinyl		1	14½″ × 24″ (36.25 cm × 60 cm)

instructions

1. Following manufacturer's directions, center and iron fusible vinyl to wrong side of top.

2. On one short edge of each bottom piece, turn up ½″ (1.25 cm), then 1″ (2.5 cm), forming a double-fold hem. Press and stitch in place (fig. 7-27).

3. Stack top and bottom pieces, right sides together, matching outside raw edges. Hemmed center back edges will overlap. Using ½″ (1.25 cm) seam allowance, stitch around outside edge (fig. 7-28).

4. To make box corner, fold corner into a point, matching seams. Stitch 1″ (2.5 cm) long seam across end, then trim off point (fig. 7-29). Repeat for remaining corners.

5. Turn cover right side out and insert foam pad. To keep pad from slipping, use a nonskid mat underneath.

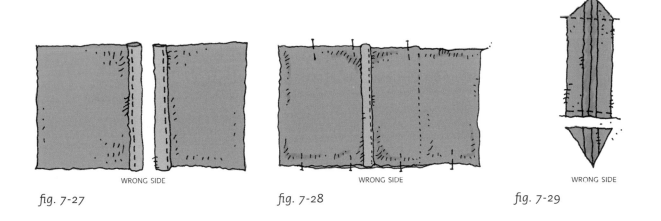

fig. 7-27 WRONG SIDE

fig. 7-27

WRONG SIDE

fig. 7-28

WRONG SIDE

fig. 7-29

Baby's Special Day
The Christening

8

Make this beautiful christening gown and accessories for Baby's special day. Embroidered dresser scarf, place mats, and doilies are used to give a Victorian look to gown, bonnet, and quilt. A memory book, easily assembled with moiré fabric, a lace place mat, and a purchased album, will provide a lovely scrapbook for photographs and mementos from this precious day.

fabric suggestions

Use cotton batiste, cotton/poly batiste, Swiss batiste, lawn, or voile for the gown, slip, and quilt. Use faille, taffeta, satin, decorator fabric, upholstery fabric, or polished cotton for the album cover.

christening bonnet

Make this fancy bonnet from an embroidered place mat. (A matching one is used for the gown sleeves.)

Supplies

Fabric	Amount
Embroidered cotton place mat	12″ × 18″ (30 cm × 45 cm)
¼″ (0.75 cm) wide double-faced satin ribbon	1½ yards (1.4 meters)

Cutting

Fabric	Piece	Cut	Size
Place mat	bonnet	1	6½″ × 12″ * (16.25 cm × 30 cm)

*Cut from the 12″ (30 cm) end of the place mat, making use of the finished edges.

instructions

1. To make sure bonnet will fit Baby, measure from earlobe to earlobe, across top of head. The average head size is about 14″ (35 cm), so adjust size of embroidered place mat as needed to fit.

2. It is likely that place mat is too narrow. If so, make bonnet extensions by cutting 6½″ (16.25 cm) from remaining end of place mat (fig. 8-22a), then splitting this piece in half crosswise (fig. 8-22b). Add to outer edges of opposite end, adjusting for width as needed to fit Baby. The object is to end up with three finished edges (fig. 8-23).

3. Layer main bonnet over extension pieces, right sides up. Stitch on top along edge of main piece, then trim away excess from back (fig. 8-24).

4. The three prefinished edges will become front and sides of bonnet. Finish as for Baby Bonnet, Chapter 2, Steps 3–5, page 25. Adjust to fit by tying ribbon to make back opening larger or smaller.

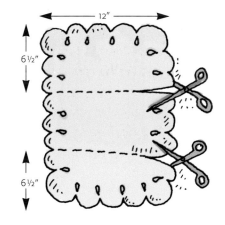

fig. 8-22a

fig. 8-22b

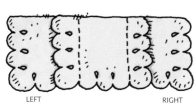

LEFT   RIGHT

fig. 8-23

fig. 8-24

memory book cover

• •

To commemorate Baby's special day, make this beautiful cover for a photograph album. Moiré fabric is trimmed with a lacy crochet place mat.

Supplies

Fabric	Piece	Amount
A	cover	¾ yard (0.75 meter)
Fusible interfacing		⅓ yard (0.3 meter)
Crocheted place mat		12″ × 18″ (30 cm × 45 cm)
Purchased photo album		10¾″ × 18″* (27 cm × 45 cm)

*The instructions apply to any size album; adjust measurements as described.

•measuring for album cover•

Determine finished cover size by measuring height (top to bottom) and width (side to side—from front edge, around spine, to back edge). Add 1½″ (3.75 cm) to each measurement. For inside flaps, height is same as cover height; width is 14″ (35 cm).

Cutting

Fabric	Piece	Cut	Size
A	outside cover	1	12¼″ × 19½″ (30.75 cm × 48.75 cm)
	inside flaps	2	12¼″ × 14″ (30.75 cm × 35 cm)
Fusible interfacing		1	12″ × 19″ (30 cm × 47.5 cm)

instructions

1. Position iron-on interfacing on wrong side of outside cover. Fuse in position (fig. 8-25).

2. If place mat is smaller than cover, position as desired on the cover, then sew. If place mat is larger than cover, add it at Step 6.

3. Fold flaps in half crosswise, wrong sides together. Pin (fig. 8-26).

4. Layer flaps on top of outside cover, right sides together, matching raw edges. Using ½″ (1.25 cm) seam allowance, sew around outside edge of album cover (fig. 8-27).

5. Turn right side out. Press (fig. 8-28).

6. If place mat or decorative item is larger than cover, position, then sew, letting edges hang over. It is important to sew as close to edge of cover as possible (fig. 8-29).

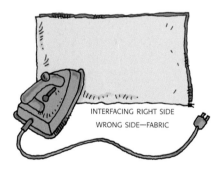

INTERFACING RIGHT SIDE
WRONG SIDE—FABRIC

fig. 8-25

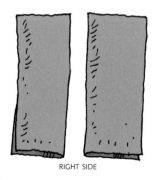

RIGHT SIDE

fig. 8-26

RIGHT SIDE   RIGHT SIDE

fig. 8-27

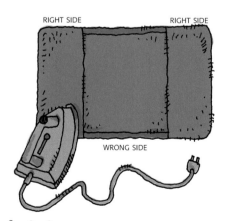

RIGHT SIDE   RIGHT SIDE

WRONG SIDE

fig. 8-28

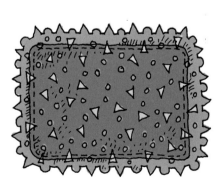

fig. 8-29

heirloom christening quilt

Battenburg lace doilies are appliquéd to this quilt for an old-fashioned look.

Supplies

Fabric	Piece	Amount
Cotton batiste	top, back, ruffle	3½ yards (3.2 meters)
2" (5 cm) wide double-finished-edge lace		9½ yards (8.8 meters)
Fusible batting		1½ yards (1.4 meters)
Nine 9" (22.5 cm) round Battenburg lace doilies		
Four 6" (15 cm) heart-shaped doilies		

fig. 8-30

Cutting

Fabric	Piece	Cut	Size
Batiste	top	1	42" × 42" (105 cm × 105 cm)
Batiste	back	1	44" × 44" (110 cm × 110 cm)
Batiste	ruffle	8	2½" × 44" (6.25 cm × 110 cm)

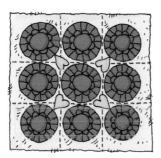

fig. 8-31

instructions

1. Mark squares by folding batiste in thirds, then again in thirds. Finger press (fig. 8-30).

2. Open up fabric and pin purchased doilies in the center of each square (pin wrong side of doily to right side of fabric). Pin smaller heart-shaped doilies at each intersection (fig. 8-31).

3. Stitch doilies in place, using a straight stitch near edge.

4. Iron fusible batting to wrong side of quilt top. Then place top on back, right sides out. Baste carefully, then outline quilt through all layers, following design in doilies (fig. 8-32). Do not quilt within 3" (7.5 cm) of outside edges of quilt top.

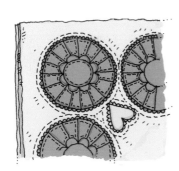

fig. 8-32

•tip•

Gather each section of ruffle separately. In case gathering thread breaks, it will be easier to redo one section than entire ruffle.

•tip•

The secret to basting ruffles with pins is to be generous. Use lots of pins.

5. Square up quilt and trim edges. Round off corners (fig. 8-33).

6. Using French seams, sew ruffle sections together to make one long strip (fig. 8-34).

7. Place lace on top of ruffle strip, wrong sides together, edges even. Stitch ⅛″ (0.5 cm) from edge (fig. 8-35).

8. Open lace to right side. Raw edge of fabric will be hidden under edge of lace. Topstitch along inside lace edge, encasing raw edge of fabric (fig. 8-36). Trim away frayed threads before topstitching.

9. Using French seam, join ruffle ends to make a circle. Using a long machine basting stitch, sew two lines of stitching along raw edge. Lines should be ⅜″ (1 cm) apart and within seam allowance. Mark center and quarter points, then pull threads to gather fabric (fig. 8-37).

10. To avoid having ruffle seams at quilt corners, mark 10″ (25 cm) on either side of each corner. Position ruffle seams at these marks (fig. 8-38).

11. Spread gathers evenly between seams, allowing extra fullness at corners. Pin and stitch to top only (fig. 8-39).

12. Trim batting ½″ (1.25 cm) from the outside edge. Working from back side of quilt, fold backing over edge of batting, then slipstitch quilt back to quilt top, covering ruffle seam (fig. 8-40).

fig. 8-33

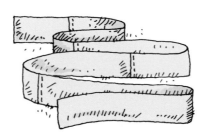

fig. 8-34

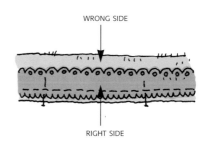

WRONG SIDE

RIGHT SIDE

fig. 8-35

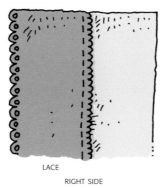

LACE

RIGHT SIDE

fig. 8-36

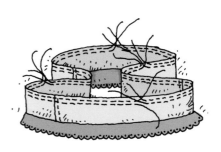

fig. 8-37

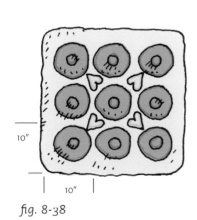

10"

10"

fig. 8-38

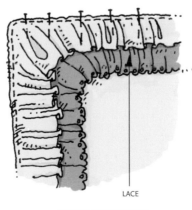

LACE

RIGHT SIDE OF QUILT TOP

fig. 8-39

QUILT BACKING

fig. 8-40

Appendix A
Sewing Basics

The following sewing techniques will help you complete the projects in this book with ease. This section is not, however, intended to be a complete guide for beginners. The topics are listed in alphabetical order.

binding

Binding is the strip of fabric used to cover the raw edges. Binding is usually cut on the bias so that it has more ease, but binding can be cut on the straight grain, too. You can either cut your own binding or use purchased binding. Making your own is easy enough, and you can choose any fabric or color you wish. The binding yardage given for each project is the total needed, whether purchased or made by you.

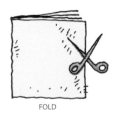

fig. S-1

corners

round corners

These have distinct advantages. Round corners (on pillows) can be turned right side out easily. Quilt binding on a round corner is eased, not mitered. To round off corners, draw a curved line—freehand or using a saucer as a template—then cut (fig. S-1). You can trim each corner separately, you can stack sections and cut through all layers at the same time (fig. S-2), or you can fold your fabric in fourths and trim all corners of one piece at the same time (fig. S-3).

You will need to ease bias binding somewhat when attaching it along a round corner. If the bias is stretched too much, the corner will "cup."

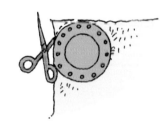

fig. S-2

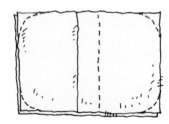

FOLD

fig. S-3

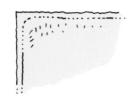

fig. S-4

square corners

Square corners (on pillows) can be tricky to turn right side out. Rather than sew a right angle, sew two to three stitches across the diagonal of the corner (fig. S-4). Trim the corner; turn right side out.

mitered corners

See Quilting Basics, page 107.

corners and ruffles

Adding ruffles at corners can be tricky. These guidelines will help.

- When pinning ruffles around corners, be sure to add extra fullness at each corner.

- Take care that the ruffle seam is along the side, not at the corner.

- When sewing ruffles around a square corner, you can round off the corner slightly with a few stitches. When turned right side out, the corner will still look square and the ruffle will drape better.

fusibles

Fusibles include iron-on interfacing, iron-on vinyl, and paper-backed fusible webbing (Wonder Under is one brand). Cut the iron-on 1/4" (0.75 cm) smaller than the fabric piece so that it won't stick to the ironing board—or press the fusible onto a larger piece of fabric, then cut to desired size.

using iron-on vinyl

Iron-on vinyl comes in matte or glossy finish. Follow the manufacturer's directions to fuse to fabric. When sewing vinyl, pin sparingly and carefully. After sewing, press the fabric side, and the pinholes in the vinyl should disappear.

using paper-backed fusible adhesive

Follow the manufacturer's directions carefully. The basic process is to draw or trace a design onto the paper side. Leaving the paper attached, iron the adhesive side to the wrong side of the fabric. Cut out the fabric shape, then peel away the paper. The shape is ready to be ironed and fused to a background fabric.

Remember that drawings for letters and numerals must be reversed so that they will read correctly when cut from fabric.

gathering

You will gather fabric when making ruffles, puffed sleeves, and full skirts.

1. Set machine to longest possible stitch length.

2. Stitch two lines ⅜" (1 cm) apart, making sure each line is sewn within the seam allowance and leaving long threads at the beginning and end of each line.

3. Pull the bobbin threads to gather the fabric.

hems

Hemming is the process of turning up an edge, then stitching it in place by hand or machine. The projects here are hemmed using one of the following methods:

- Single-fold hem: Finish the raw edge using one of the methods described on page 111. Turn up and press. Stitch by machine through all layers.

- Double-fold hem: Turn up raw edge ¼" (0.75 cm), then ½" (1.25 cm). Press and stitch by hand or machine along folded edge.

hemstitch

Use this machine stitch to finish the join of lace and fabric. The end result looks like small hand buttonhole stitches.

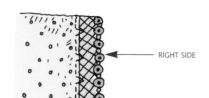

fig. S-5

1. Insert a wing needle into sewing machine. This needle has a wide shank and will make a hole at each stitch.

2. Set machine for blanket stitch. Adjust the stitch width so that the needle swings from lace to fabric over the fabric roll (fig. S-5).

lace

The roll-and-whip technique allows you to attach lace to the very edge of the fabric.

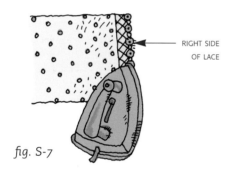

fig. S-6

1. With right sides together, place lace along fabric edge, leaving ¹⁄₁₆" (0.25 cm) of fabric exposed. (The edge must be clean, with no frayed threads hanging off.)

2. Set machine to narrow zigzag; the stitch should catch the lace header and sew just over the raw edge of the fabric. As you sew along the edge, the zigzag stitch will roll and whip the edge of the lace header and fabric together (fig. S-6). (Start with a stitch width of 3 and stitch length of 7, then adjust as needed. If too many "little fuzzies" appear, shorten the stitch length.)

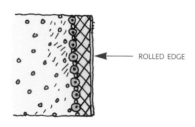

fig. S-7

3. After sewing, open lace away from fabric and press hem toward fabric (fig. S-7). Hemstitch if desired.

piping

Covered piping makes an attractive finish for pillows and other items.

1. Following the project instructions, cut bias strips wide enough to wrap around cording plus 1".

2. Fold bias lengthwise over cord, with right side out and raw edges matching.

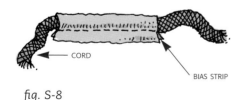

fig. S-8

3. Using a zipper foot, stitch immediately next to the cord through both layers of fabric (fig. S-8).

pressing

Press seams as you go. Seams ½" (1.25 cm) or larger should be pressed open. Quarter-inch seams should be pressed in one direction because they are too small to open. On pieced quilt tops where seams need to nest, press seams in opposite directions.

raw edges

Baby items are laundered frequently, so all seam edges need to be finished. Test one or more of these methods on a scrap piece of fabric, then select the one you like best.

- Cover raw edges with a machine overcast or zigzag stitch. This is recommended if your fabric ravels easily.

- Trim raw edges with pinking shears.

- Use a serger to trim and overcast edges in one step.

seams

- To join separate pieces of fabric, place them right sides together, matching the raw edges. Then stitch along the raw edge using the recommended seam allowance.

- To enclose the raw edges inside the seam, use a *French seam*. With wrong sides together, stitch a ¹⁄₁₆" (0.25 cm) seam. Press (fig. S-9). Turn so that right sides are together, then stitch again, using a ¼" (0.75 cm) seam and enclosing the raw edges inside the seam (fig. S-10).

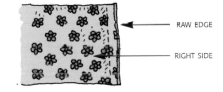

RAW EDGE

RIGHT SIDE

fig. S-9

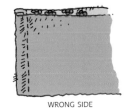

WRONG SIDE

fig. S-10

Appendix B
Quilting Basics

This section covers basic techniques you'll need to complete the quilts in this book.

Quilts have three layers—the top, the batting in the center, and the quilt back. The process of sewing through all three layers—by hand or machine—is called quilting.

quilt top

Detailed piecing and/or appliqué instructions are given for each project.

quilt back

You will usually have to do some minimal piecing for the bottom layer, or backing, of a quilt because it will be wider than a standard width (42"–45"/105–112.5 cm) of cotton fabric. Muslin, flannel, and decorator fabrics can be purchased in larger widths.

Try this technique for making wide fabric. Cut two lengths. Split one down the middle, and sew each half to the outside of the first length (fig. Q-1). Be sure to trim off selvages before joining.

Since the quilt back doesn't show, you can use unmatched fabrics from your stash. Leave the backing larger than the quilt top and batting. After the layers have been quilted, square up the sides and trim all layers to size.

fabric suggestions

broadcloth

cotton

calico

gingham

decorator fabric

Projects shown use seven coordinating fabrics.

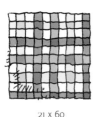

21 x 60
FIRST LENGTH

fig. Q-1a

30 x 60
SECOND LENGTH

fig. Q-1b

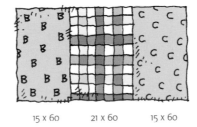

15 x 60   21 x 60   15 x 60

fig. Q-1c

batting

Batting is the middle layer in a quilt, and it is held in place with quilting stitches. Follow manufacturer's guidelines for specific quilting recommendations. In general, cotton batting should be quilted at 1½"–2" (3.75–5 cm) intervals. Polyester batting doesn't shift as much as cotton batting and doesn't have to be quilted as closely. Polyester is also more hypoallergenic.

The puffiness is called loft, and most battings are labeled high-loft or low-loft. Either is fine, but low-loft is easier to work with.

Some battings have a glazed finish which makes machine sewing easier. The finish minimizes "bearding," the tendency of batting fibers to poke through the fabrics. When sewing fabric and batting together by machine (see Bumper Pads, page 8), place the batting on the bottom and fabric on top. The glazed side of the batting will be next to the feed dogs; the fabric will be next to the sewing foot.

basting

A common question is how to hold the layers of a quilt together so that you can quilt without getting puckers in the top or backing. The answer is to baste with brass safety pins.

Place the quilt backing right side down on a hard, flat surface, such as a large cutting table or a tile or wood floor. Center the batting, then center and layer the quilt top, right side up (fig. Q-2). (The pieced top is usually the smallest layer; the backing is the largest.) Working from the center out, smooth out large wrinkles and puckers until all layers are positioned properly.

Starting in the center and working toward all four edges, pin the layers every 4" (10 cm) to form a grid (fig. Q-3). Continue to smooth the layers while pinning. Gently pull the bottom layer occasionally to ease out any puckers.

Safety pins are essential—the quilt will be handled a great deal during the quilting process and straight pins will fall out or get lodged in the batting where they might prick Baby later. Brass safety pins are best—their sharp points and smooth finish slip easily through the fabric.

If you prefer traditional hand quilting, simply hand baste a grid of long lines a few inches apart. Work from center to outside edges, both top to bottom and side to side. Basting threads are removed after quilting is completed.

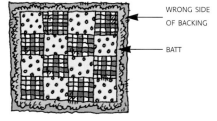

WRONG SIDE OF BACKING

BATT

fig. Q-2

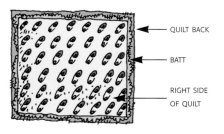

QUILT BACK

BATT

RIGHT SIDE OF QUILT

fig. Q-3

quilting stitches

Quilting stitches add a subtle texture and dimension. You can quilt by hand or machine, using thread that contrasts or matches. Choose a contrasting color if you want quilting stitches to show; use a neutral or matching color if you want your stitches to be more subtle.

If you are quilting a traditional pattern, you can draw (or trace with a stencil) the design on the quilt top with lead pencil or soluble ink, then quilt on the drawn lines. Other methods of quilting include *outline quilting* (outline motifs with stitches), *echo quilting* (repeat the outline several times, but each repeat is a few inches away from the previous one), *stipple quilting* (free-motion quilting, usually by machine, in a pattern of squiggly lines that do not cross), and *stitch in-the-ditch* (stitch in or next to a pieced seam).

quilting by machine

A crib-sized quilt is ideal for machine quilting because of its smaller, easy-to-handle size. To minimize the tendency to sew in puckers and pleats, hold the fabric with both hands to keep it taut as it goes under the needle.

Machine quilting tends to make fabric layers shift while being sewn. An evenfeed foot will help, but you should also change directions—sew one line from top to bottom, then turn the quilt and sew from bottom to top. Depending on the quilting design, you can also alternate right/left directions with top/bottom directions.

As you sew, hold the layers firmly. Grasp from the top with your left hand behind the machine needle; grasp from the underneath side with your right hand in front of the machine. Take care to ease top and bottom layers carefully because they will tend to pleat and pucker at each seam crossing. The top layer is visible, of course, but by grasping firmly, you will be able to feel the bottom layer and ease it where needed.

quilt binding

See binding, page 101.

•tip•

When stitching in Step 5, the fabric will be unwieldy, but keep going. Once the stitching is complete, the fabric will form a neat tube.

1. Start with a square of fabric (a 36″ [90 cm] square will make more than 16 yards [14.8 meters] of 2″ [5 cm] wide bias).

2. Cut diagonally from corner to corner (on bias) (fig. Q-4).

3. Pin the two halves right sides together, matching the raw edges along the straight grain. Stitch, using a ¼″ (0.75 cm) seam allowance. Press the seam open (fig. Q-5).

4. Mark the width of the bias parallel to the bias edge (fig. Q-6).

5. With right sides together, match the bottom edge (BAB) to the top edge (DCD), offsetting by the desired width of the bias (fig. Q-7). Stitch, then press the seam open.

6. Starting at the marked end, cut the bias strip, measuring as you go (fig. Q-8).

7. Using a bias pressing device, pull the bias through the device and press the edges toward the middle (fig. Q-9).

A fabric square this size	will make approximately this much 2″ (5 cm) wide bias
15″ × 15″ (37.5 cm × 37.5 cm)	2¾ yards (2.6 meters)
26″ × 26″ (65 cm × 65 cm)	9 yards (8.3 meters)
34½″ × 34½″ (86.25 cm × 86.25 cm)	16 yards (14.8 meters)

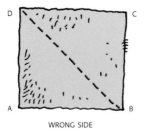

fig. Q-4

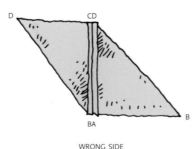

fig. Q-5

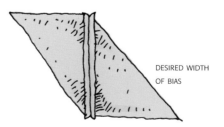

fig. Q-6

attaching bias binding

Detailed instructions are given for each project, but the general procedure is as follows:

1. Trim all quilt edges with a rotary cutter and ruler, making sure the sides are even and square.

2. Pin the bias binding to the front of the quilt, right sides together and edges matching. Pin carefully about every 4″ (10 cm). Work on a flat surface so you don't accidentally pin in any wrinkles.

3. Sew through all layers to hold the binding in place.

4. Fold the binding to the back of the quilt, covering the raw edges. Slip-stitch the binding in place along the back.

An alternate method is to sew binding to the back, fold it over the raw edge to the front, then topstitch in place by machine on the front.

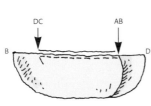

fig. Q-7

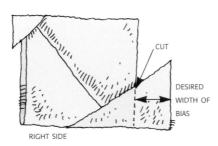

fig. Q-8

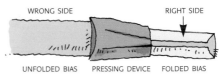

fig. Q-9

mitered corners

Here is an easy way to make a mitered corner when attaching bias binding to a quilt.

1. Starting in the middle of the bottom edge of the quilt, place binding on the front of the quilt, right sides together and edges matching.

2. Stitch, stopping several inches away from the corner. Mark ¼″ (0.75 cm) from each corner with a pin (fig. Q-10).

3. Sew to the first pin; lock stitch. Measure 1″ (2.5 cm) of binding; mark with a pin (fig. Q-11).

4. Match the pin on the binding to the second corner pin. Lock stitch, then continue sewing (fig. Q-12).

5. When the bias binding is turned over to the back, the corner fold will be mitered (fig. Q-13).

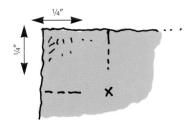

fig. Q-10

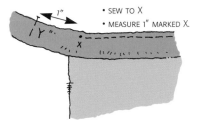

fig. Q-11

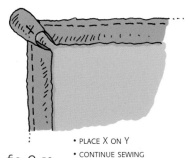

fig. Q-12

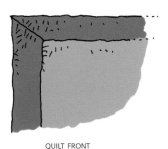

fig. Q-13

hanging sleeve or rod pocket

Make a sleeve, open on both ends, and attach it to the top of the quilt back. Insert a curtain rod through the sleeve and the quilt is ready to hang on a wall.

1. Determine the unfinished width of the quilt (do not include binding). Cut a strip of fabric 2" (5 cm) shorter in length than this measurement and 9" (22.5 cm) wide.

2. Make a double-fold hem on each end by turning up ¼" (0.75 cm), then ½" (1.25 cm). Press and stitch to secure each end.

3. With wrong sides together, press in half lengthwise to form a long tube.

4. If the quilt is not yet bound, sew the sleeve onto the top edge of the quilt back, stitching through all layers in the seam allowance. Bind the quilt. Secure the bottom edge of the sleeve to the back of the quilt with slipstitches.

5. If the quilt binding is already in place, stitch along the lengthwise edge to make a sleeve. Press the tube, centering the seam on the back side of the sleeve. Pin the sleeve in position on the back of the quilt. Secure the top and bottom edges with small invisible slipstitches.

Patterns

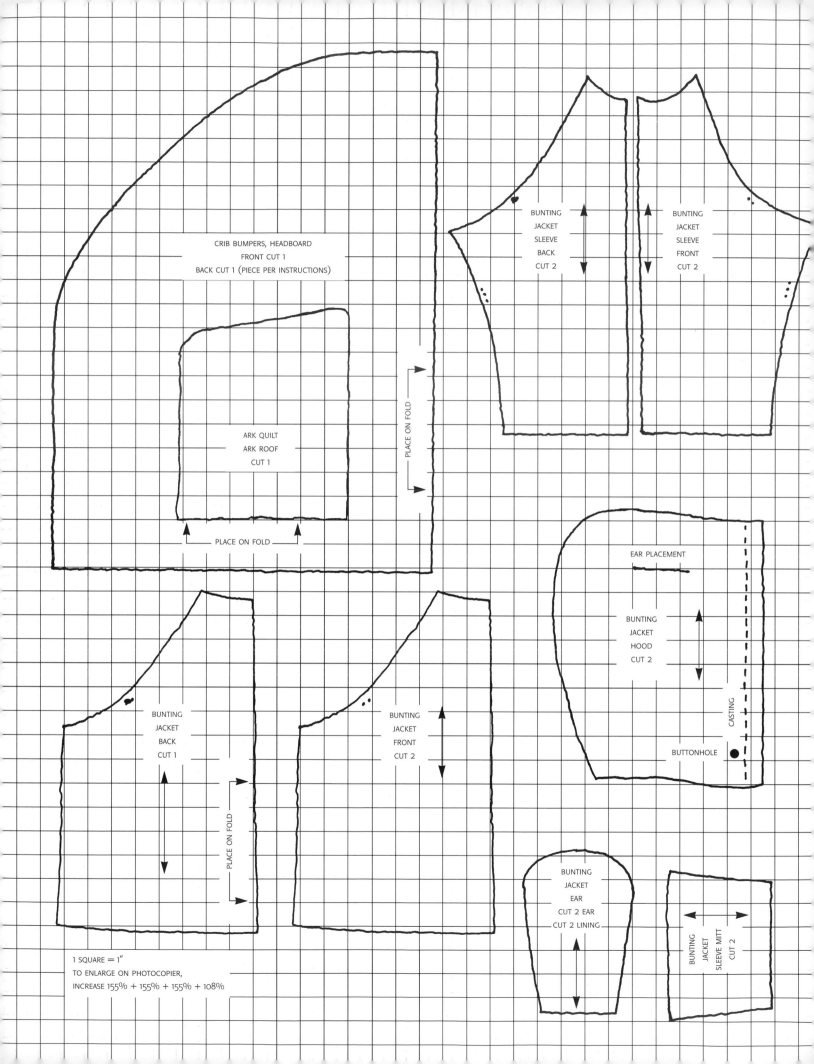

CRIB BUMPERS, HEADBOARD
FRONT CUT 1
BACK CUT 1 (PIECE PER INSTRUCTIONS)

BUNTING
JACKET
SLEEVE
BACK
CUT 2

BUNTING
JACKET
SLEEVE
FRONT
CUT 2

ARK QUILT
ARK ROOF
CUT 1

PLACE ON FOLD

PLACE ON FOLD

EAR PLACEMENT

BUNTING
JACKET
HOOD
CUT 2

CASTING

BUNTING
JACKET
BACK
CUT 1

BUNTING
JACKET
FRONT
CUT 2

PLACE ON FOLD

BUTTONHOLE

BUNTING
JACKET
EAR
CUT 2 EAR
CUT 2 LINING

BUNTING
JACKET
SLEEVE MITT
CUT 2

1 SQUARE = 1"
TO ENLARGE ON PHOTOCOPIER,
INCREASE 155% + 155% + 155% + 108%

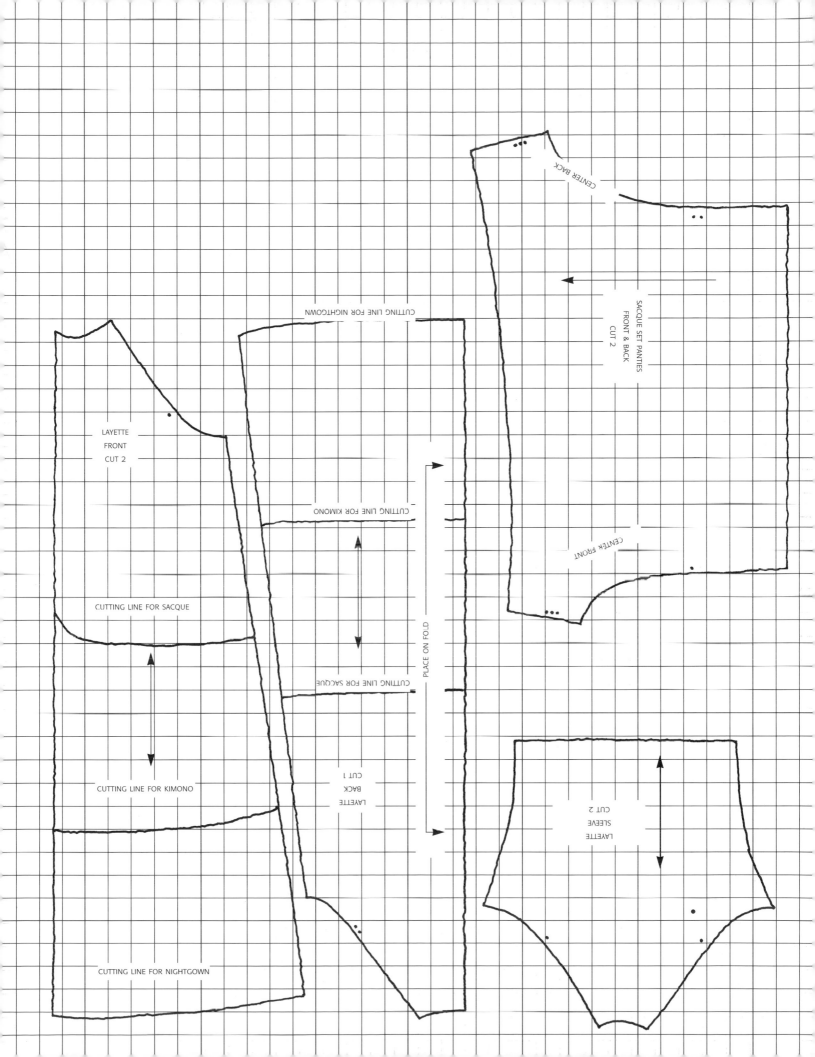

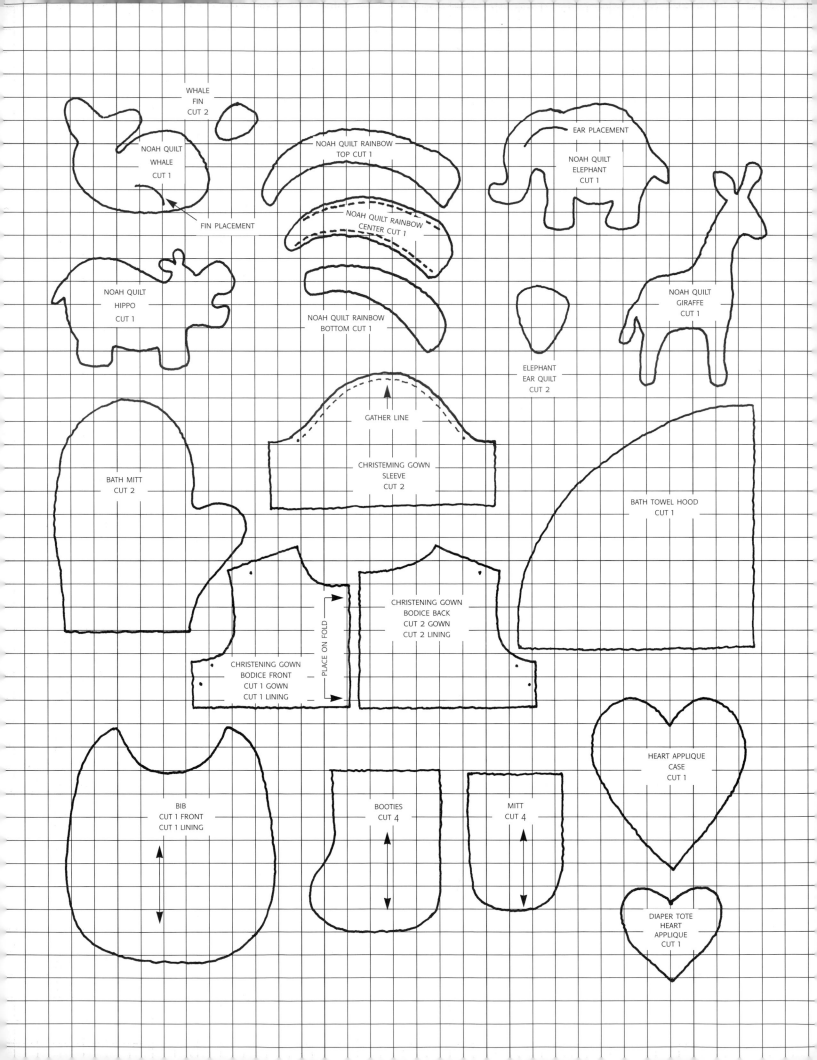

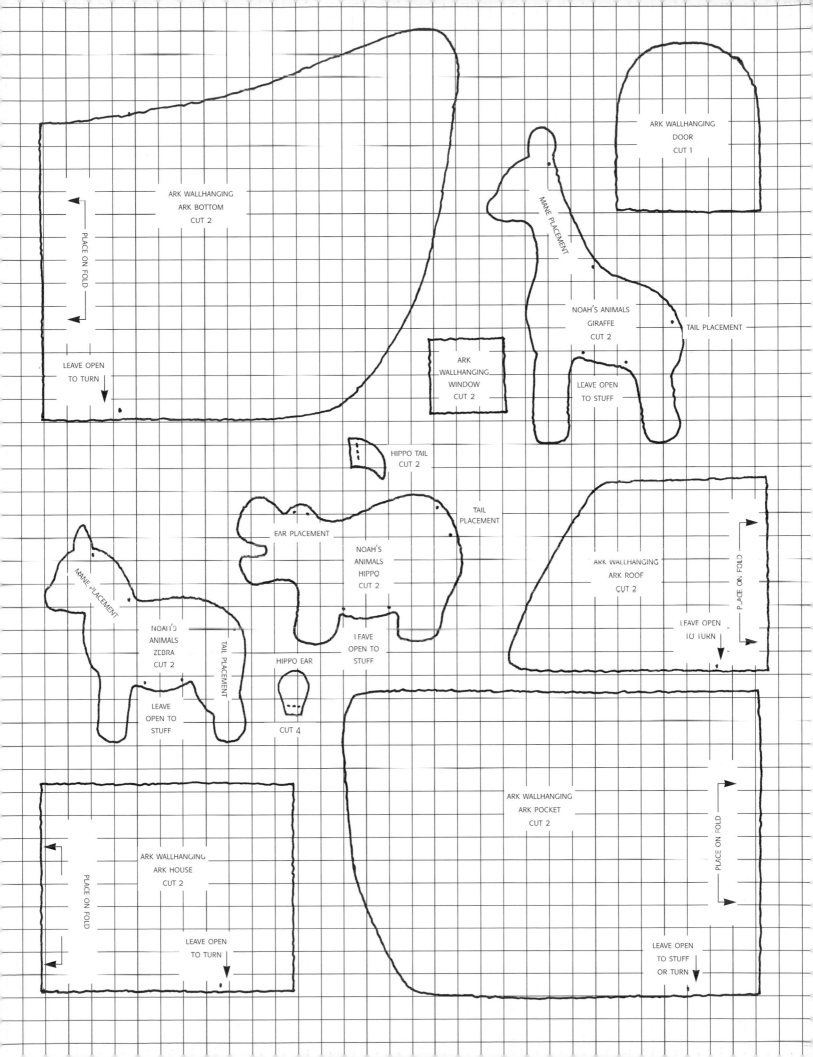

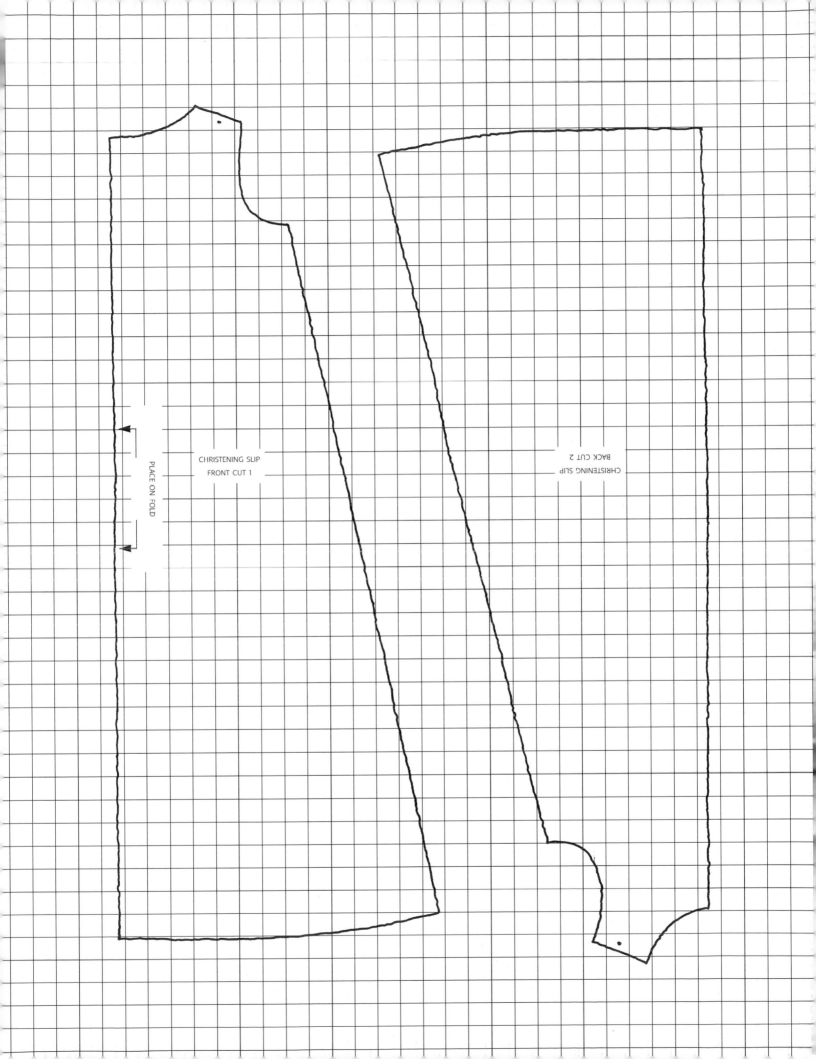

CHRISTENING SLIP
FRONT CUT 1

PLACE ON FOLD

CHRISTENING SLIP
BACK CUT 2

Notes

Notes

Notes

Notes

Notes

Notes